www.ingramcontent.com/pod-product-compliance
Lightning Source LLC
LaVergne TN
LVHW061944070526
838199LV00060B/3961

Find us on the web: https://wordpeddlersociety.com

POST-APOCALYPTIC

2023 Book Recs — January Vol 1- Issue 1

Written by TheWordPeddler
December 29, 2022

Welcome to the WordPeddler's Society Book Recs
Week of — January 1st

Check out some of our favorite apocalypse reads for this first week of the year

Author Menu

Writers on Writing
Resources
Submit A Book
Author Listing

Post Categories

Select Category

Groups

Newest | Active | Popular | Alphabetical

Sci-Fi Epic Reads
Active 5 months, 1 week ago

Spicy Books
Active 5 months, 1 week ago

Written Apocalypse
Active 5 months, 1 week ago

Asylum of Fear
Active 6 months ago

Written Undead
Active 6 months ago

We wanted to kick off our new book blog with some recommended books for our readers and friends. 2022 is coming to an end and we are all working hard to move forward into the next year. Coming in 2023 is more from the WordPeddler's Society. Here it is all about the books, the authors that write them, and the readers who love them. Coming in the year ahead you can get these sent straight to your mailbox, find them on social media or just come to the site and check out what is on for the week in your favorite genre. As it expands we will see books in all genres and the posts will be tagged with the genre so you can simply go to that category to see all of the books throughout the year. We plan to bring you featured titles on sale as well as the releases for the month.

Happy reading!

Recent Posts

Restricted content
Writers on Writing with Jeff Thomson
WordPeddler on the Hero's Journey – Vol 1 – Issue 4
WordPeddler on Why I'm a Writer – January 16th
WordPeddler on Authors as Readers — January Vol 1 Issue 3

Recent Comments

Pat O'Dell on 2023 Book Recs — January Vol 1- Issue 1

BUY SHARE PREVIEW   BUY SHARE PREVIEW   BUY SHARE PREVIEW

BUY SHARE PREVIEW   SHARE PREVIEW   BUY SHARE PREVIEW

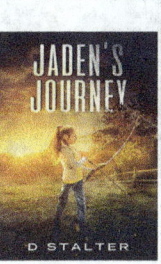
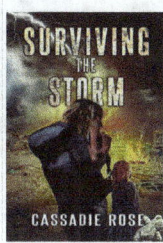
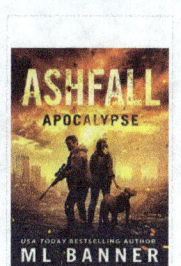

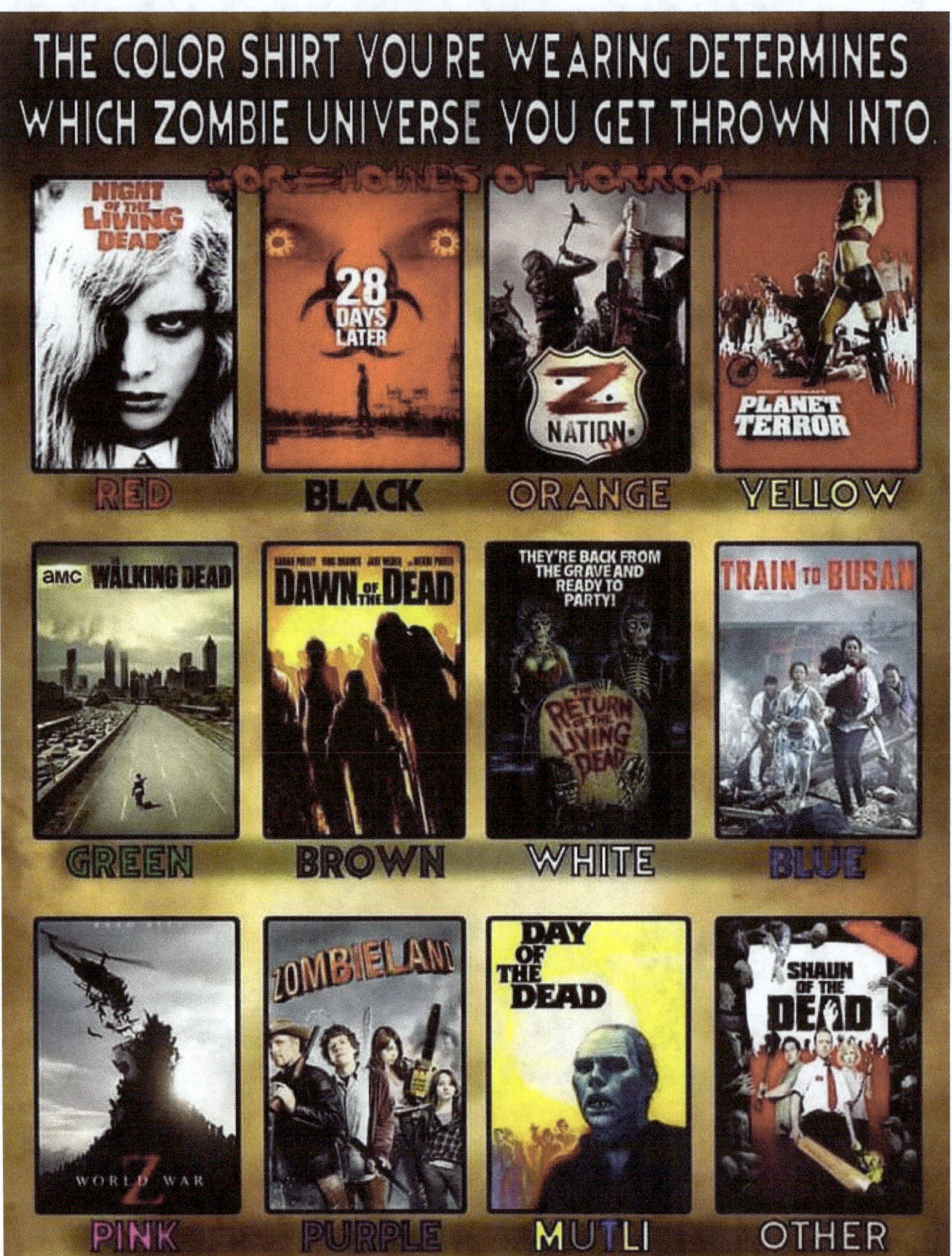

Classifieds

Beyond The Fray
Publishing

Manuscript Editing

Fiction | Nonfiction

Flat rate $.002 per word

Contact @dauntlesscoverdesign.com

Raventhorne Books

Bitter Mayhem:
Dakota Destruction Book 1

After a series of coordinated attacks devastate the United States, Katie and Leo sacrifice everything to help their country.

Katie was one semester away from a degree in graphic design, living a carefree life with her boyfriend Leo.

Then the apocalypse happened.

Place your AD Here

For rates and information Contact

Admin@angryeaglepublishing.com

KYLA STONE
RIVETING APOCALYPTIC THRILLERS

LUNATIC, FATHER, AUTHOR

◊ World Made by Hand — by James Howard Kunstler

This book is set long after the apocalypse and chronicles the way communities might evolve post-apocalypse it details some of the tasks and jobs community members might take on and outlines many interpersonal relationships while continuing to show the strife and problems humans might still face. We recommend this book as not only an amazing look into what comes after but also a feel-good story because after all it can't be just surviving, we also need to thrive.

◊ Alas Babylon — by Pat Frank

The main protagonist, Randy Bragg, was given a brief warning of the coming nuclear war by his brother, who was a member of the Air Force. Randy had enough time to buy supplies at local stores but did not fully realize what was useful and what was not in a disaster until after the attack. Aside from the effects of the radiation or the luck of being upwind of the blast, Alas, Babylon exposed weaknesses of modern living in an unpowered society. Randy and his small community had to figure it out the hard way. t The favorite thing we learned was "iron rations" and how important something like this is.

◊ Lights Out — by David Crawford

There are those of us that recall watching this book evolve on Frugal Squirrel, a forum that saw chapters loaded. We all on the forum offered thoughts and feedback, but this is likely our favorite of the list for one reason… The Karate Man. This is not as you might think, it is the way the author portrays a very real and relatable character. He reminds us in this book about the importance of teaching our skills to others or they may be lost forever.

◊ 1984 — by George Orwell

Who doesn't love a good Orwellian dytopian adventure? We sure do… While this is not actually an apocalyptic book but one about a Dystopian Future, we think it is a great read to remind us of what could be with an overpowering goverment in the hands of a few bad people. An enjoyable read that makes you think what if?

TOP APOCALYPTIC READS

We polled the groups and asked the question...What books got you into the apocalypse?

AND THE RESULTS WERE...

◊ One Second After — by William R. Forstchen

What's not to be said about this book? This book was written as a warning to Congress about the dangers of an EMP, but fast became a classic that convinced many people to become preppers. If you want to have a real look into what it might look like, look no further. We can learn a lot about the realities of this very real threat to our society.

◊ The Stand — by Stephen King

A cult classic about "Capt'n Tripps" a plague that decimates most of the world's population. There is the good ole' battle between good and evil, but this one hits the list for its entertainment value. There are lots and lots of great apocalyptic books out there but nothing beats characters such as "trash can man" or "Flagg." If you understand what M-O-O-N spells, you've likely been a fan of this book as well.

◊ Lucifer's Hammer — by Larry Niven & Jerry Pournelle

A massive comet breaks apart and bombards the Earth, with catastrophic results: worldwide earthquakes, volcanic eruptions, thousand-foot tidal waves, and seemingly endless rain... With civilization in ruins, individuals band together to survive and to build a new society. Another classic that reminds us that it isn't always just one thing we need to prepare for but that often disasters can kick off others.

About the Author

Sadly, we lost Christi this past year. She was an enthusiastic writer who sought to learn all she could. She wrote for every opportunity offered and her light for this art never faded.

Christi Reed grew up helping her mother and grandmother garden and can food. She could remember all the hours of prepping vegetables to be canned. When her grandmother died, they stopped doing as much gardening, but those early memories stayed with her. She's always loved to read and tried a couple of times to write but never had the confidence to do anything with it.

Coming in 2023 Look for Christi's novel published posthumously
HOMESTEAD REVIVAL

Read more of these stories in Apocalyptic Winter
An Angry Eagle Anthology

Warning!
A book so cold you might freeze your Apocalypse off!

Enter twelve different worlds where survivors must face the end of civilization as they know it, all while battling the brutal and deadly elements of Winter.

AMAZON.COM/DP/B082GN9M83

As the weather continued to warm, we filled all the empty cans we had saved and filled them with dirt. It was time to try starting some of the seeds they had salvaged. If we could get them started inside, we had a better chance of a healthy garden this summer. Spring had always been a sign of new beginnings for me. It stood for a time of rebirth and new growth.

We were all outside trying to clear and dig up an area to use for a garden when our next visitors appeared. At first, we didn't recognize them. They were no longer bundled up in winter gear.

"Hello, the cabin." They called from the edge of the tree line. "We were out this way and thought we'd see how you were doing."

"Hello, nice to see friendly faces after all this time." Sherry called out as she realized that these were the two men who had taken the last raider away. "Did you find the women you were looking for?"

"We did. They had been abused and were in bad shape, but we think they will be ok. They are back with their families now." One of the men answered. "Looks like you're working hard, need any help?"

"We're just trying to get the ground ready for a garden. We really don't know very much about how to go about it though. Well, granny does, but the rest of us are pretty clueless." Seth replied. "We mostly lived in town before the power died."

"We can give you a hand with that. Do you have seeds to plant? My name is Mark and this guy is Tom." he said, gesturing to his companion.

"We have some seeds that we salvaged from empty houses. Not sure if it's enough or a good variety. Some things we have a lot of if you need some." Sam offered.

Mark looked over, "We could trade some work on your garden for the extra seeds that you don't need, if that sounds fair to you?

Sam grinned, "Not sure about that, sounds like we are getting the best part of that deal."

The men took over the heavy digging while the kids got in the way trying to help. At least that was the excuse they gave for playing in the dirt. We, being smart women, sat back and listened to them chat while they worked. At one point where they mentioned trips into town, I spoke up. "If you see canning jars and lids on your trips, we could use more of them. Canning vegetables and extra meat would be easier than trying to dry all of it."

Mark nodded, "We'll see what we can find. We could trade canning lessons for the jars if we find them."

"We can do that even if you don't find any more jars. I would be happy to pass on some of the knowledge I have. You know at one point this winter I almost gave up and let myself die because I couldn't see how an old lady like me could be of any use in this new world." I commented. "It seems like a miracle to me that there is something I can do to make life better now."

The End...

When one of the kids outside let out a yell, we were smart enough not to go running out the door.

Looking out the window, we saw 5 scruffy looking men standing in the yard. While not fat by any means, these five also didn't look like they had missed many meals. Considering how hard food was to find in this new reality, that meant that they could only be raiders. We knew we didn't have long before they tried entering the cabin.

"Ladies, this is what we will do." I quickly laid out a plan. I truly hoped that none of our group would end up being injured. We couldn't just aim at driving them off, because raiders would just keep coming back.

"Come out of there!" The leader yelled. "If you don't come out, we will kill this boy and then come in after you."

"You can't get us all before the men get back here." I yelled back.

"We know your men are gone. We watched them leave this morning. All we want is you women and the food." He said that as if it wasn't a death sentence.

My job was to distract him and try to get the boy away. Jerry was a good kid and I wasn't willing to let him die for the rest of us. I stepped out onto the porch, making sure to keep the pistol in my hand hidden in the folds of my clothing. That was easier than it would have been a few months ago. My clothing hung on me now only held up by the string I used for a belt.

I knew that I had to get closer to them. I wasn't a very good shot with the pistol. I walked down the steps and moved toward them.

"That's far enough, granny! You're not the women we are after." The leader said with a leer.

I took another step and pretended to stumble, bringing the pistol up and shot for his chest. I didn't wait to see if I had actually hit him. I grabbed Jerry and fell to the ground. As I did all the women inside shoved rifle barrels out the windows and shot towards the men.

We used a lot more bullets than we probably should have, but none of us were used to using the guns. When the shooting stopped and we had time to look around, we counted four of the raiders on the ground. One had gotten away. We were all still in shock over what we had done, when we heard clapping.

Looking toward the sound, we saw two men with rifles slung on their backs at the edge of the trees. It took some time to realize that they also had the other raider on the ground.

"Good job! We've been tracking this bunch for a couple days. They raided another house a couple of miles from here." One of the men said. "If you don't mind, we'll take this one with us. We need to find where their base is and see if the women they took are still alive."

"Please take him! If the women need help, we would be glad to do what we can." Sherry spoke up. "Our men should be back soon, and they can help clean up this mess."

"You did the right thing. It is hard to take a life, but we are basically reduced to old west rules at the moment. It's kill or be killed out there. Hopefully, it will get to the point where we can form communities again." One of the men reassured us before they left.

We were all still sitting on the porch staring at the dead bodies when the men got back from hunting. None of us could stand the idea of touching the bodies. We were still trying to deal with the idea that we had killed other human beings.

The men took care of stripping the bodies and dug holes to bury them. Everyone was quiet that night. Each of us was thinking about how the world had changed. It was slowly getting better. However, as that day had shown we still needed to be cautious. As the days passed, we also remembered that there were other good people out there, just like us they were trying to survive.

I didn't used to remember my dreams, but it seemed like lately dreams were all I had, and they were much better than this reality.

I woke, or thought I did, to warmth and the sound of people talking. Someone held a warm cup to my lips. Tea! It had been so long since I had tasted tea, and it was sweet! I slowly sipped from the cup as I fought to open my eyes. I was sure that I was still dreaming and didn't really want to wake up.

"Drink just a little more, you need the liquid. We were almost too late in finding you." A voice I'd never heard before said. I felt myself being lifted and propped up so that I was almost sitting. I was on something soft and my hip didn't hurt like it did most mornings in the cold.

"Where am I? Who are you? Am I still dreaming?" I had to know if I was finally losing my mind.

"Easy, it's ok, you're safe here." A deep voice tried to soothe me. "We have been looking for people who ran like you did. We are banding together to try and get through this."

I finally got my eyes open enough to see that I was in a log cabin lit with candles. There was what looked like a huge fire in a fireplace. As my eyes moved past the fireplace to the other side of the room, I couldn't believe my eyes. "Is that a Christmas tree?"

For some reason this made everyone laugh. One young woman answered me, "Yes, you're not dreaming or crazy. We think its December now, so we wanted to try and keep some of the traditions for our kids. We don't have fancy lights or presents but that's not really what Christmas started out as anyway. We're just celebrating having made it this long."

"How long has it been? I've lost track of so much time being all alone." I still wasn't really sure if any of this was real.

"We think it's been about 5 months since the lights went out. It's only in the last few weeks that things have started to settle down." A young man answered as he put his arm around the woman I'd been talking to.

"I'm sorry it took us so long to find you, but it really wasn't safe before now to try looking."

"You have nothing to be sorry for. Thank you very much for taking a chance looking at all. Is there anything I can do to help here?" I really didn't like to feel useless after having to do everything by myself.

"You don't by any chance know how to fix a turkey do you? We managed to kill one earlier but none of us really know how to get the feathers off it. We've been living off the food we had stored and salvaged from deserted houses. None of us are very good with hunting and cooking." The young lady asked.

"As a matter of fact, I do know how. We will need a big pot of boiling water to scald the bird before we pluck it."

Imagine that! There were some things that older people could help with. Maybe there was a place for me in this world of survival after all.

As everyone sat eating turkey and rice that evening, I thought back to all the holiday meals of the past. The wooden serving spoon would have been a sterling silver serving spoon at those meals, but the wooden one worked just as well, and looked like it was hand carved.

I spent a lot of time that winter teaching the youngsters how to prepare food, cut up game, and how to knit and sew. It felt almost like having my own children back again. Even though we were getting low on food, I made them save some of the potatoes for seed in the spring. When they went out on salvage trips, I asked them to look for canning jars and the lids for them. They had seen them but didn't know how to use them.

In the evenings after dinner we would all sit and talk about what they needed, and what needed to be done in the spring. For the first time since the power died, I found that I was looking forward to the spring. For now, we were busy planning. Hopefully we could find the seeds we would need for a garden in the spring.

The days were finally getting a bit warmer. We were getting more sun and fewer storms. We had sent the men out to hunt. Warmer weather, while good for all of us, meant that it would be harder to keep meat from spoiling. We women were trying to get the inside of the cabin cleaned and organized as much as possible. It was the closest we could get to spring cleaning, perhaps.

FROM THE ARCHIVES
YOU'RE NEVER TOO OLD

By Christi Reed

I sat as close as I could get, next to the wood stove, desperately trying to absorb some of the heat. I knew that there was very little chance that I would survive until spring. In fact, it was hard to believe that I had made it this long without being killed.

I thought back on what had happened because even that was better than thinking about how very cold, I was. When the power suddenly went out, the world had gone totally crazy. People who had been friends and neighbors, suddenly became predators. I knew the only way to survive was to get as far away from any other people as I could.

I found an old backpack that one of the kids had left behind when they moved out. I shoved all the food I could into it. I filled it with bags of rice, dried beans, baking mix, and anything else I could fit in it. I knew it was going to be heavy, probably more weight than I had carried in the last 10 years, but I couldn't waste any food. There were still canned goods and bottled water. I needed to find another way to carry the rest. In the attic I found one of those suitcases with wheels on them so you could pull them. I managed to pack most of the rest of the food into it and waited for darkness. There was no room to pack clothing in the bags, so I put on everything I could layering it one thing on top of another.

When it was dark enough to hide, I snuck out of the town. I had a destination in mind. When we were kids, playing in the woods, we had found what we called our Secret Play House. It had to have capitals because it was so cool.

It had taken me all night to reach it. It never seemed like it was that far away from the house when we were kids. When I finally saw it in the early morning light, I was amazed at how good our childish imaginations had been. Our Secret Play House looked a lot more like a falling down sap shack to me.

As bad as it looked, it was still some shelter from the elements. I poked my head inside and saw that the small wood stove was still there where I remembered it. Putting the bags inside I curled up on the hard, dirty boards of the floor and slept. For weeks I gathered fallen branches to use for firewood. I used mud and moss to plug as many holes in the walls as I could. There were still leeks in the woods and a few black berries still on the bushes. I found some walnuts and acorns that the squirrels had missed. I gathered what I could, every little bit I found was important.

I thought about trying to make it back into town to try and find more food or bedding, but I wasn't sure that I could make it there and back. The arthritis in my knee and hips had made the trip out here torture. I didn't think I could force myself to do it twice. When the weather got colder, I piled fallen leaves and moss in the corner for a bed and covered up with a knitted scarf. It didn't offer much warmth, but every little bit helped. Getting old had been hard enough before the end of the world, now it was it was pretty much a death sentence. More than once I wished that I could just hibernate through the winter like a bear. Sleeping through the cold winter months to awaken in the spring sounded like a great idea.

It was peaceful all alone in the woods, but lonely. I had never been much of a people person, but I really missed my books. My mind sometimes wandered, and I would find myself remembering some of the stories I had read.

I hoped that my children had found somewhere safe, but there was no way to check on them. I wondered sometimes if dying would be such a bad thing. This survival stuff seemed like it was something for younger people to try. I remember reading somewhere that freezing to death was a peaceful way to go. You just got cold and fell asleep and never woke up. Still, I wasn't quite ready to give up yet.

I lost track of the months. At first, I had tried to track time by making marks on the walls with a rock for each day. After a while it just didn't seem all that important.

Once in my dreams I thought I heard bells and people talking, but I knew it had to be a dream.

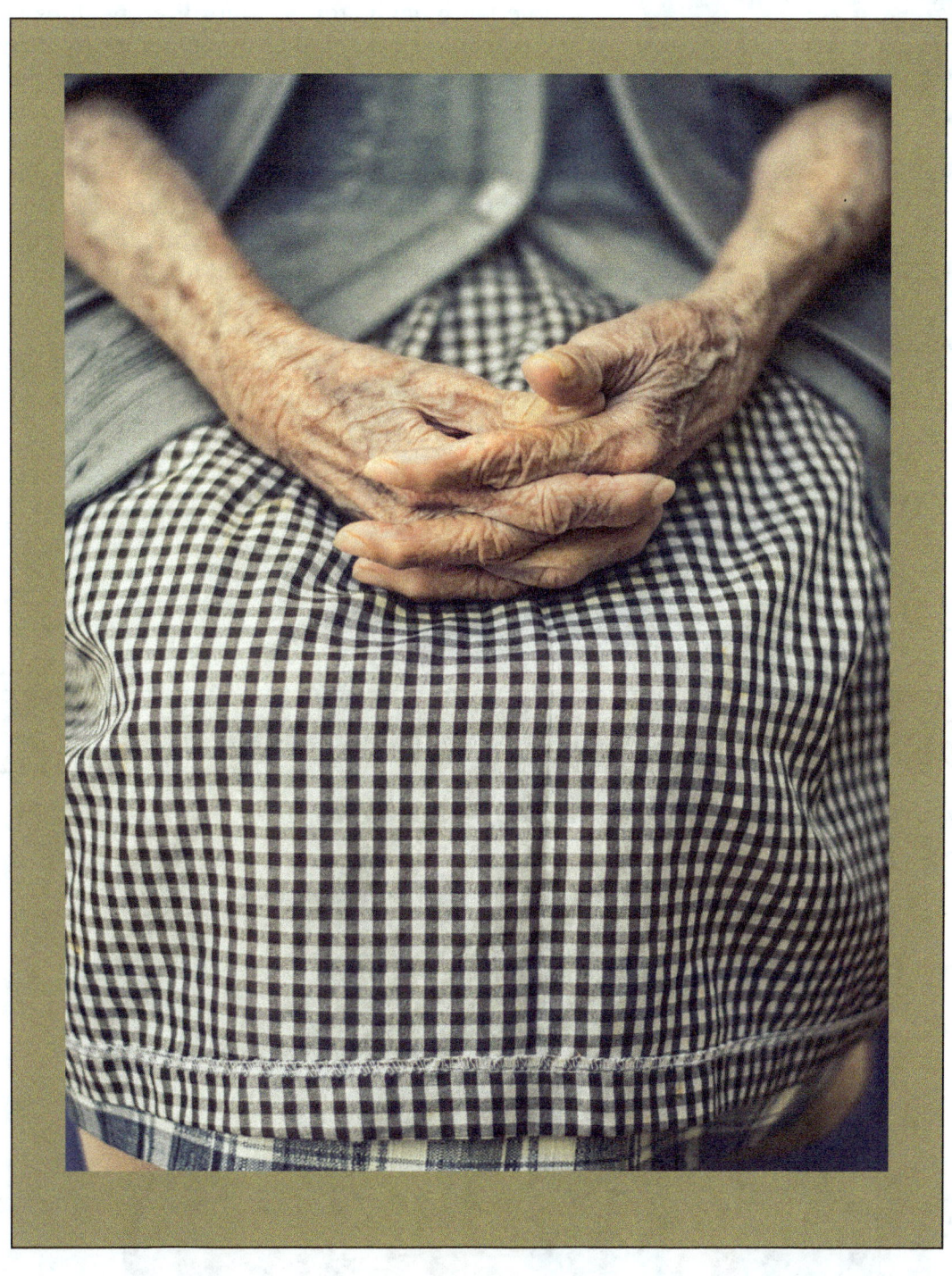

About the Author

A fourteen-year veteran of the USCG, Jeff Thomson served as a navigator on four different ships and as SAR Controller at two Group Operations Centers. He is currently retired from his life as an over-the-road truck driver, which was not the most conducive writing environment, and yet, he managed to write the majority of his first novel, a bit of his second, and a chunk of his third, using his steering wheel as a desk. He is now writing full time (on an actual desk), and currently working on the second and third books in his Epic Mayhem series.

THE FIRST EIGHT BOOKS of his Guardians of the Apocalypse zombie series AVAILABLE IN AUDIO VERSIONS, PLUS MATTHEW CROW'S HILARIOUS RENDITION OF SCREAM BLOODY CHEERLEADER. CHECK THEM OUT ON AUDIBLE.COM

Follow me on Twitter: Jeff Thomson@JSThomson2021

Find His Books

https://www.amazon.com/stores/Jeff-Thomson/author/B07BBL72YD

So a certain degree of fear makes sense. We also know flying is statistically safer than driving a car (particularly in you live in Los Angeles), so if the fear causes problems in a person's ability to function in modern society, then it means they have issues. In this case, it has long been established that the phobia is actually masking a fear of not being in control. Understanding this, then, is the gateway to eliminating the issue.

With me so far?

To finally get to the point, what this means to us as writers of fiction is that it doesn't matter how bizarre we make our characters behave, provided this behavior makes sense to them and it remains psychologically consistent throughout the story. Allow me to provide you with three examples: Stephen King's Trashcan Man, from The Stand, JK Rowling's Luna Lovegood, and Thomas Harris's Hannibal Lector.

Trashy is certifiable. No doubt about it. So much so, he spent time at the nut hatch in Terra Haute, where he received shock treatments after setting fire to Old Lady Semple's Social Security check. He hears voices and has visions. At no point in the story does he seem as if he's playing with a full deck. At the same time, however, what he does always makes sense to him. He never questions it, and neither do we.

Luna Lovegood is quite possibly my favorite character in the Harry Potter saga. The girl is an unashamed and unapologetic wing nut. She, also, never questions it. If anything, she leans into it, and we are left to shake our heads in entertained wonder. We believe her character.

And then there's Hannibal the Cannibal. Talk about letting your crazy out to play! He appears in three different novels, and remains consistent throughout. At no point do we question whether or not he questions his own behavior. I doubt any of you reading this knows what it's like to be a cannibal from personal experience. At least I hope not. If you do, kindly keep your fava beans away from me. Be that as it may, however, we enjoy his character because we know he enjoys being himself.

So there you have it, my two cents worth on the psychology of character. I can expand on this at a later time, if you like, but for now, this will do. As always, I look forward to your thoughts and comments.

WRITER'S CORNER

PSYCH 666; THE PSYCHOLOGY OF CHARACTER

by Jeff Thomson

The psychiatrist (and Scotsman) R. D. Laing once said schizophrenic behavior makes sense to the schizophrenic, or words to the effect. He also said "Life is a sexually transmitted disease and the mortality rate is one hundred percent," so perhaps we should take his words with a grain of salt. Be that as it may, what he meant was that no matter how bizarre or unhinged a person's behavior might seem to those not so afflicted, somewhere deep inside the cosmic soup of their psyche, it makes sense to them.

Pulling ourselves back from the brink of drooling insanity, any psychological quirk one may have, such as a fear of flying, can be understood if we figure out what underlying purpose it serves to the person who has it. The fear can be regarded as rational (to a degree) in so far as one is zipping through the air at several hundred miles per hour while trapped inside a metal tube, and if God meant for us to fly he'd have given us wings.

About the Author

N.A. Broadley is a mother of two grown children, two grandchildren, a wife, and a homesteader. She has a passion for writing funny homesteading stories along with post-apocalyptic fiction. She lives and fights with a rooster named Peckerhead, who makes it his mission to make her life as interesting and as challenging as it can be.

From a small homestead in Southern New Hampshire, in a small log cabin, N.A. Broadley shares with you her love of prepping, homesteading, and her books based on the premise of 'What if?
Follow her on Amazon
amazon.com/stores/N.A.-Broadley/author/B07V282K4K

Read more of these stories in Anarchy
An Angry Eagle Anthology

Beware!
this book is smoking hot —

Welcome to the Apocalypse!Enter thirteen stories where survivors must face the end of civilization as they know it, all while battling the brutal and deadly anarchy that is all too inevitable.

AMAZON.COM/DP/B08D6W3CYL

"Yes, I'm afraid I'll end up burning this shit," she replied, handing Danny a package of freeze-dried chicken stew. Danny read the directions and dumped the entire contents into the pan, added the appropriate amount of water, and waited for it to boil. Once it came to a rolling boil, she turned the heat off and covered the pot.

"Five minutes and it should be ready," she murmured. "Why don't we sit at the kitchen table," she suggested. Lifting the pot from the stove, she carried it into the kitchen, picked up Billy, and sat her on one of the chairs then set the table. By the time she was done, the stew was ready.

The package only made a few servings. Shawn noticed that Danny took a very small spoonful for herself, then dolloped a larger amount for Billy and Shawn. Shawn shook her head and grabbed the spoon from Danny. She scooped some from her plate back onto Danny's.

"There's more than enough," she murmured. She watched Danny's eyes fill with gratitude.

"Thank you, Shawn, you've kept my baby from having to go to bed hungry tonight," she whispered, gazing deep into her eyes. Shawn felt her face blush with warmth.

"Hey, we ladies gotta help each other out, right?" she teased, not wanting Danny to see the tears burning her own eyes. In all the chaos of the last few days, all the fear she'd swallowed down and the panic she'd kept just below the surface, for this moment, Shawn felt like she'd found comfort.

Chapter Five

They talked long into the night, sitting by a stub of a candle between them on the coffee table in front of the couch. Billy, sleeping peacefully with her head resting on Danny's lap.

"So where were you going?" Danny asked quietly. Shawn smiled and shrugged her shoulders.

"Away from the city, toward Washington. I have a friend there," she replied. Then turning her eyes to Danny, she asked,

"And you? Is there a husband?" She saw Danny grimace and shake her head.

"No, I was only sixteen when I got pregnant. The father, scared shitless, bailed out on me. So, it's just been me and Billy," she replied. The shadows moved in the room with the flickering candlelight, dancing off of the corners and the walls. Danny sighed worriedly.

"So, what now? Do you suppose things will get back to normal soon?" she asked. Shawn shook her head.

"I don't know. I saw the Army coming into Manchester yesterday. The fighting was fierce, but I don't think they could hold the city. That's why I ran. So much violence and bloodshed," she muttered.

"Yeah, I saw that today too in Hooksett, at the store, just before I was taken," Danny replied. She brushed her hand across Billy's hair and hitched back a sob.

"What'll happen to all of us?" she whispered. Her voice filled with pain.
Shawn gulped hard around a lump in her throat before answering.

"We will survive, we will make it!" she hissed. "We have to! You've got her to take care of, to keep safe, we will do what we need to!" She watched Danny nod.

"I killed a man last night and you know what? I didn't hesitate. And you can't either," Shawn murmured. Danny's eyes widened in horror and she nodded. To protect her baby, hell yes! She would kill.

Just then, Shawn heard a soft growl from the rooster. She placed her finger across her lips, motioning for Danny to stay quiet. Grabbing her knife from her pack, she stood and walked toward the window and peeked out. She saw the silhouette of a truck parked in front, on the street.
Turning to Danny she whispered, "One-second advantage,"
Danny raised the gun and aimed. When the door flew open, she pressed the trigger.

The End...

"You are crazy, woman!" she said then snickered. "Give me that damn gun and I'll load it," she finished, holding out her hand. Shawn grinned and handed it to her. Stopping, she put her pack on the ground and dug out a box of bullets.

"Will these fit?" she asked. She saw Danny roll her eyes and smile.

"Yes, they fit," she replied as she loaded it. "This gun is nice, it's a Ruger, 1911. Easy to handle," she said. "Just point and fucking shoot," she murmured, handing the gun back to Shawn. She pushed her hand away.

"No, you carry it. I've got my knife," she replied. Guns made her nervous. Loaded guns scared her. She thought about the steak knife and the attack on her the night before. Yes, she'd much prefer a knife. It wouldn't accidentally go off and shoot her foot off.

"Okay, we're here," Danny murmured as she rushed toward a two-story Victorian-style house. Shawn and the rooster followed her up the front steps.

"Baby? Baby, where are you?" Danny yelled as she made her way through the front door. Shawn watched a small girl come out from behind the couch.

"Oh baby, come here," Danny sobbed as the little girl rushed into her waiting arms. Shawn heard the rooster behind her squawk. Turning she shooed him away.

She saw Danny stand, pulling the little girl up with her.

"Shawn, meet Billy," she murmured. A pair of golden-brown eyes stared at her from a pudgy round face. Shawn smiled.

"Hi Billy," she said warmly. The look of pure love on Danny's face as she held her daughter melted Shawn's heart. How could there be so much violence, so much anger, and hatred in the world when this love was so evident? It almost broke her heart thinking about it.

Setting her pack on the floor, Shawn wearily glanced at the couch.

"Oh, my gosh, sit Shawn," Danny said. Setting the child down she motioned for Shawn to rest.

"I can't thank you enough for what you did for me today. That was very brave of you," she murmured, glancing at Billy, her face filling with a mixture of fear and sadness.

"No thanks needed. I'm just glad I was there," Shawn replied. The soft cushions of the couch felt heavenly under her dragging ass.

"Oh, do you have water? We've got a few different meal choices, but they all need water to cook them with," Shawn asked. Reaching for her pack, she slid it toward her. Flipping the top flap, she pulled out several freeze-dried meals.

"I do have water. Just before the power went out, I filled the bathtub and several containers. But how are we going to cook those?" Danny asked. Shawn smiled and pulled out the little rocket stove.

"On this," she replied with a grin. Danny's eyes lit with excitement.

"Sweet! Let me go get some water and a pan," she replied. Shawn saw the concerned look she cast to Billy.

"I know baby, you're hungry. It'll be a few minutes and we'll get that tummy full," she murmured. Shawn nodded and turned to the little girl.

"Do you want a candy bar while you wait for dinner?" she asked, her voice teasing. She laughed when Billy nodded shyly.

"Okay, here ya go," Shawn said and handed Billy a chocolate chip granola bar. Her eyes widened when she saw her tear into it hungrily.

"Whoa, slow down, you'll choke kiddo," Shawn chided as she watched Billy's cheeks puff from overstuffing her mouth.

As Billy ate her bar, Shawn got the little rocket stove lit. Danny brought in a tin pot and a container of water and set it down on the coffee table.

"Okay, want me to help?" she asked. Shawn nodded. She wasn't really a good cook.

"Leave! Climb in your truck and just leave, okay?" she said, her voice shaking. "I don't want to have to kill you," she pleaded. She nodded as she watched him back toward his truck.

"I'll come back, ya know. And when I do, you will pay," the man hissed as he climbed behind the wheel and fired up the engine. Shawn kept her gun pointed at him until he spun away.

After he left, she let out a whoosh of breath. Turning to the woman, she gave her a quick once over.

"You okay?" she asked. The woman grimaced as she wiped the blood from her lips.

"Yeah, I'll live, thank you, by the way, he would've killed me," she muttered. Shawn nodded. Of that, she had no doubt.

"What happened?" she asked. She watched as the woman's face crumpled with tears.

"He took me from the grocery store. I was trying to find a few things to feed my daughter, we are out of food and she is so hungry," she replied, choking back a sob. Shawn shook her head.

"That's horrible, how far away do you live?" she asked. The woman turned her face toward her.

"About two miles that way," she said as she pointed up the road.

"Okay, I'll walk with you home, I've got a little bit of food I can share," she replied. The woman again started bawling.

"Thank you, thank you," she replied. Shawn smiled.

"Let me go get my pack, it's just over here in the woods," she muttered as she walked back to where she'd dropped her pack. The woman followed behind and Shawn heard a chuckle when she saw the rooster sitting calmly beside Shawn's pack.

"Yours?" she asked. Shawn grinned.

"I guess, he's sorta adopted me," she replied as she bent and hoisted the pack to her shoulders.

"I'm Shawn," she said then held out her hand. The woman grasped it tightly.

"I'm Danny, nice to meet you, Shawn," she replied.

Chapter Four

It took them several hours to walk the few miles to Danny's house. Shawn was tiring quickly, and her slow pace became even slower. Glancing sideways at Danny, she grimaced.

"So that creep that took you... he doesn't know where you live, does he?" she asked nervously. Danny paused her step and looked at Shawn.

"No, I mean I don't know him but fuck, he's got my purse. Inside of it is my driver's license with my address," she groaned. Shawn sucked in a quick breath.

"Damn it, let's pick up the pace, how much further you think?" she gasped as she pushed herself to move faster. Danny shrugged her shoulders.

"Maybe a half-mile," she muttered as she tried to keep up with Shawn's faster pace. As they walked Shawn kept an eye out for the man's truck. His promise to come back rang in her ears and fear trembled through her body. If he came back, would she be able to bluff her way out again? Would he bring others? All sorts of horrid images flashed through her mind, ramping up her anxiety.

"Do you know how to shoot a gun?" she asked breathlessly as she pushed her tired body through the woods at the edge of the road. Danny turned to her.

"Yes, why? Do you have an extra?" Danny asked. Shawn couldn't help but laugh bitterly.

"Nope, only the one. But I've no idea how to even load it!" she muttered. Danny stopped, her eyes wide and her mouth forming an 'O' of surprise.

"You mean back there... that fuckin thing wasn't even loaded?" she squeaked. Shawn nodded.

"Nope, it was all a bluff," she replied. "I had a one-second advantage and took it," she finished. Danny hooted with laughter, her eyes filling with tears.

Bringing it to the living room she set the cup down on the floor.

"Okay bad boy, your turn," she muttered. She glanced at the window. The sun shone brightly through it.

"Shit, we gotta get outta here," she muttered. She was talking to a freaking rooster! Smiling at this thought, she made her way back to the pile on the floor and repacked the backpack. Once done she made her way into the kitchen and rifled through the cupboards for a container to carry water in. She found a quart-sized water bottle on the very top shelf. Pulling it down, she filled it from the water heater and tucked that into one of the side pockets of the backpack.

"You coming?" she asked, glancing down at the rooster. With that, she opened the door and stepped out into the morning.

"We got miles to cover, bad boy," she murmured.

Chapter Three

The day grew hot and Shawn found herself stopping more than she had planned to. Her breath hung heavy in her chest as humidity made breathing difficult. Sweat beaded her forehead and she swiped it away with a dirty hand. Rather than walk the road, she chose to walk the edge of the woods. This way she could dart in and run if she encountered trouble. It was funny, she thought she would see more people fleeing the cities. But in the several hours, she'd been walking, she saw no one. Well, no one except for the rooster who followed behind her like a puppy. Sighing, she slipped into the woods a bit further, still keeping the road in her sight, and found a tree to rest under. Sliding out of the heavy pack, she winced. The straps had rubbed raw spots on both her shoulders.

"I need to rest," she muttered, glancing at the rooster. She watched as he settled himself on the ground a few feet away. The sound of a racing engine alerted her to traffic out on the road. Standing, she peered over a cluster of brush and watched as a truck sped up then slammed on its brakes, coming to a halt in the middle of the road. She listened and watched from her hiding spot as a woman about her age jumped out of the passenger side and screamed. The man driving the truck, a big, burly looking dude, flew out of the driver's door and ran toward her. Shawn's breath trapped in her throat as she watched the woman fighting the man off. She winced in horror as she saw him raise a fist and drive it into the woman's face.

"Get back here, you bitch!" he roared, grabbing a handful of the woman's hair. Shawn cringed when she saw him throw the woman to the tar, her face skidding along the pebbly grit.

"Shit! Oh shit!" Shawn moaned. Fear rooted her feet to the ground as the woman's screams split the air. Anger pulsed right behind her temples. Turning, she quickly grabbed her pack, frantically searching for the gun. Grabbing it, she shouted.

"Get the fuck away from her!"

The man turned toward her as she walked out of the woods and toward him. She held the gun in the position she'd seen so many times in the movies. And prayed he wouldn't figure out that it wasn't even loaded. Gritting her teeth, she snarled angrily.

"Back away, or I swear I will fucking plant you!" she growled. The man, his eyes boring into hers, took a step backward.

"Mind your own business, Missy. This here girl and I have some unfinished business," he murmured. Shawn watched his hands as they moved toward his belt, then to his pocket.

"Don't! I swear, I will kill you," she lied. The man grinned. The woman on the ground climbed to her feet screaming,

"Shoot him! Kill this mother fucker!" Shawn cut her eyes to her then back to the man.

Her legs shook, barely able to hold her up as she stumbled to the couch and collapsed. Blood, warm and sticky, trickled from her battered nose. Her breath rasped in and out of her throat as she fought back sobs. She heard the rooster clucking low and anxiously but in the darkened room she could only make out his shadow as he danced around the dead man on the floor. Terror paralyzed her as the reality of how close she'd come to dying set in.

"I can't, I just can't do this! I don't know how," she cried. Using the sleeve of her jacket, she gingerly wiped the blood and snot from her nose. Her stomach growled, reminding her of how hungry and thirsty she was which only made her more miserable. Drawing her knees up, she stared into the darkness until the first gray shimmer of light reached its fingers through the window.

The light brought with it the starkness of the body lying on the floor. A man, full-bearded face, eyes staring lifelessly at the ceiling. Her knife sticking out of his chest as if mocking her. The rooster, settled quietly beside the body watching her. Pushing herself wearily off the couch, her body screaming with fatigue she walked over to the man and glared down at him. It surprised her at how handsome he was. A normal, everyday type of guy she would more than likely had been attracted to. But his handsomeness hid the monster inside of him. A shiver traced icy fingers along her spine. Bending, she grabbed his shoulders and dragged his body across the floor, leaving a trailing smear of blood. Why was she bothering to hide him? Well, because if someone else came along looking for him then they would probably try to find the person that killed him. And she wasn't about to take any chances.

Opening the closet door, she grunted as she struggled to push him inside. After a few moments, she finally got him settled behind a rack of hanging clothes. Standing, she took a deep breath. Her eyes set upon a backpack on the closet shelf and she reached up, pulling it down. It was heavy. Curiously, she knelt and unzipped it. She couldn't suppress the squeal of delight as she saw the contents inside. Whoever owned the house must have been a long-distance hiker. The pack was filled with all kinds of survival gear and food. Hastily she emptied it, excited as a kid in a candy store.

Her eyes widened as she looked down on the pile of booty. There were a dozen or so packages of freeze-dried meals, everything from flavored rice and noodles to Ziplock baggies filled with breakfast and granola bars. There were several dried packets of flavored drinks and some kind of straw looking thing that had LifeStraw printed on the side of it.

Along with those items was a camp kit, a small rocket stove with fuel packets, a tent, two pair of socks, some rope, a fold-up knife with multi-tool attachments, a silver sheet of material folded into a small square, a small medical kit, a toothbrush with a small tube of paste and laughing, she picked up a small battery-operated blender with a bag of chocolate frosty mix stuck inside the blender top.

Lastly, she found a handgun with several boxes of ammunition. She picked up the handgun carefully. The cold steel sent a chill through her hands. She knew nothing about guns. Had no idea of even how to load the bullets into it. Setting it back down carefully, she picked up a package of food. Glancing at the label she read the directions.

"Shit, I need water for this," she muttered. Tossing it back in the pile, she grabbed a granola bar and tore the wrapper open. Hungrily she stuffed it into her mouth, chewing and swallowing so fast that she didn't even have time to taste it.

As she ate, she frantically wandered through the house in search of water. With the power out, she knew she couldn't draw from the faucet. In the bathroom, she spied the hot water heater. Bending down she eyed the small release valve at the bottom of the tank. Smiling, she jumped up and ran to the kitchen, all the while feeling the rooster's eyes on her.

"I bet you're thirsty too," she quipped as she darted back into the bathroom with a cup. Opening the valve on the hot water heater she hooted in joy as she watched a trickle of water come out.

"Okay, we're in business," she muttered as she filled her cup. Lifting it to her lips she sucked it down in three long swallows then bent and filled the cup again.

Could she actually stab another person? The thought sent a chill coursing through her. After a few moments of seeing no movement in the cottage, she gingerly stood. She sucked in a deep breath, steeling herself. A movement in the brush behind her sent a jolt of fear through her and she turned quickly to see a huge rooster calmly gazing at her with its beady eyes. She let out a scream of terror before she could clamp her mouth closed on it. Taking a step back she warily watched it. Did roosters attack people? She didn't know.

"Shoo!" she muttered, waving her hands at it. The rooster glanced at her, blinked once then growled.

"Oh shit, really?" she hissed. She backed up a few steps.

"C'mon, just shoo!" she squawked. She watched the bird take another step toward her. Turning, she ran for the cottage. She heard the flapping of wings behind her and she dove for the front porch. Landing hard, she felt her left knee skid along the rough porch boards. Scrabbling on her hands and knees, she reached for the doorknob just as the rooster landed beside her. Frozen breath caught in her throat as she found herself face to face with the massive beast.

"Oh, c'mon Mr. Rooster, no," she moaned. She was about at her wit's end. She saw the rooster glance at her, blink, and then take a step back. Pulling herself to her feet, she kept her eyes on him.

"Okay, so, I'm going in this house, I'm going to find a place to sleep. You go away," she muttered. Her heart raced wildly as she talked to the bird and took another step. He mimicked her movement with a step of his own giving her the impression he wanted to follow. Sighing, she opened the door and watched as he scooted into the house. Stepping in behind him, she let her eyes adjust to the darkness.

Other than having no power, everything in the house appeared normal, well, as normal as could be in the situation. The first thing Shawn did was to check the cupboards and refrigerator for food. Both, much to her dismay, were empty. Groaning, she rubbed at her empty tummy. If she had to guess, she suspected that those who lived here had packed up and left. Sighing tiredly, she walked over to the couch and sat. Her body ached from the many miles she'd put under her feet. She heard the rooster in the corner scratching around. Leaning back, she closed her eyes. Weariness flooded through her and it didn't take long for her to drift into a light doze.

Chapter Two

A loud squawk woke her from a sound sleep, and she bolted up off the couch to her feet just in time to see a shadow standing over her with an arm raised. Screaming she threw herself sideways to avoid the blow which grazed her shoulder. She heard a hiss as she kicked out her foot and connected with some part of her attacker's body. Grabbing the knife from her pocket, she rolled onto the floor and came up underneath the person, driving the blade into their foot. A scream echoed through the darkened room as she crawled frantically through the dark toward the front door. She screamed in fury as she felt a hand grab a fistful of her hair and jerk her backward. Scrabbling with her hands against the floor, she felt a fingernail rip off of one of her fingers, the pain quick and stabbing. Her breath exploded as her attacker launched a boot into her ribs and she collapsed onto the floor.

"Bitch, you'll pay for stabbing that little pig sticker into my foot!" a voice growled into her ear. Numbly she felt strong hands jerk her up and she gasped as a fist plowed into her face. She felt her nose break, sending blinding pain soaring through her head.

This bastard was going to kill her! With a scream as adrenaline coursed through her, she slammed her head into her attacker's face, the explosion of pain sending white lights twinkling behind her eyes. From behind her, she heard a growl and then the flutter of wings as the rooster launched himself onto her attackers back. This gave her the one-second advantage she needed as she drove the knife still clutched in one fist deep into her attacker's chest. She heard his gasp of surprise as she twisted the blade. She choked back a sob as she watched him fall.

FROM THE ARCHIVES
ONE SECOND ADVANTAGE

By N.A. Broadley

Shawn moved along the shadows of the road, staying hidden as she walked. Times were turbulent. Her long hair was held back in a braid, the gray hood of her sweatshirt pulled up over it. She moved with purpose. Goal number one was to find a place to shelter down for the night. Goal number two was to not die before she did. The sound of popping gunshots echoed on the other side of the ridge. She winced. People had lost their minds. They had torn the cities apart, driven people like her out. She had nothing. Not even a backpack. Just ratty sneakers on her feet, torn jeans on her ass, and a will to live. She didn't even have time to be scared.

Her gaze stared straight ahead. Smoke spiraled up on the horizon and she guessed from its location that it was the small suburb on the outskirts of Manchester burning. Casting her eyes away, she glanced down and stopped in horror. Her mouth formed an 'O' for a scream, but nothing came out other than a gasp-like rush of breath. Shivering, she scooted backward a step or two to avoid stepping on the work boot lying on the tar at her feet. It wasn't the boot that sent terror crashing into her heart but the bloody hunk of foot and ankle still inside the boot. Tears stung her eyes as she choked back the urge to vomit.

"Who the fuck would do that?" her mind screamed. Skirting a wide birth around the boot, she struggled with the rise of panic that surged through her. If she lost it now, she knew she'd crawl up into a hole on the side of the road and just die. She couldn't give in to panic or give up. Biting her lower lip, she tipped her head down and marched forward.

What had happened? She'd asked herself that question at least a hundred times in the last twenty-four hours. One minute she had been curled up in her apartment, on the couch, watching television and taking stock of her last bit of groceries. Every channel carried the latest riots. Every city across the United States burning, stores looted, people being filmed, while others murdered them in the streets. What started it? Now that was the real question. No one knew. Perhaps it was the movement from the government toward martial law... perhaps it was the famine that had finally driven desperate people to do desperate things.

Hunger had a way of turning normally law-abiding citizens into panicked mobs. Either way, the city of Manchester had imploded. Her apartment was no longer a safe spot. So, gathering up what little she could, she made a run for it. She'd gotten about a half-mile when she was attacked by a group, thus losing what little she'd brought with her. Shaking her head, she quickened her step, leaving the memory of the attack behind, along with the bloody stump of the foot and ankle sticking out of the boot.

She pondered her direction. The neighboring towns, Weare, Henniker, Hillsboro, and Washington, in one direction; Concord and Nashua in another direction. She chose to head for Washington, NH. Rural, with lots of homesteads and farms. She knew of a friend out there, Dirk. Would he take her in? She didn't know, but at this point, she had no other options but to try to make it to his homestead.

She figured being on foot would take her many days to get there. She estimated the small town was, at a guess, about fifty miles away. Her stomach growled with hunger, and she pushed the discomfort away as she thought about the sparse amount of food she'd had before the attackers had taken it from her. Fucking animals! Didn't they care that she was hungry too? An image of the boot with said attached foot flitted across her mind. No, they wouldn't care that she was hungry.

People like that who could attack a person and only leave a bloodied boot behind probably didn't give a rat's ass about much.

The small cottage looked empty. More than empty, it looked abandoned. She crouched behind the bushes and watched. Shadows moved over her shoulders, the sun setting into dusk. She didn't want to be out in the dark. Too dangerous. Reaching into her pocket she let her fingers graze across the blade of the steak knife. It wasn't much for defense, but it was better than nothing.

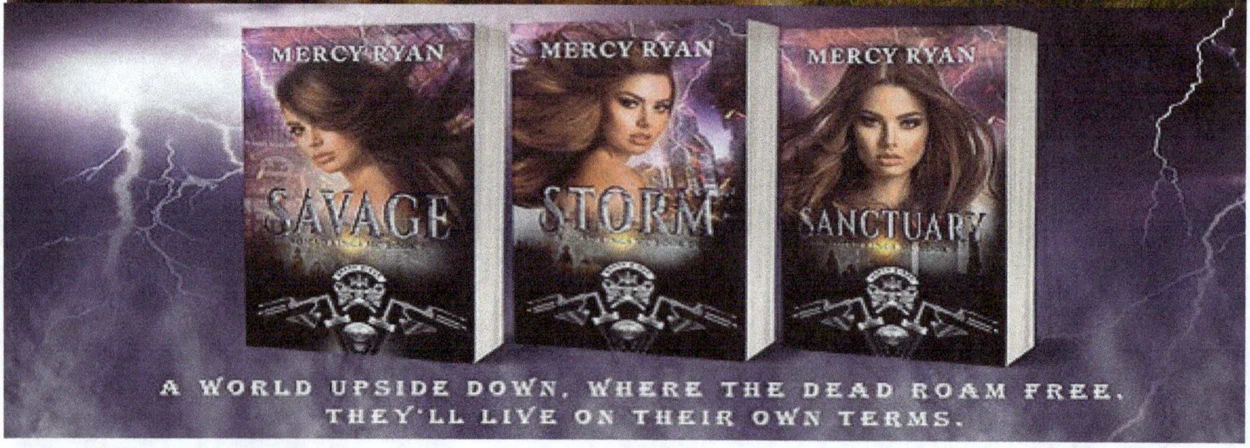

It's The End

```
G H E L E C T R O M A G N E T I C P U L S E S
L B U G O U T D W Y U R T E O T W A W K I A G
T C O Z T C D P I A E Z C J B H M B I N E R B
E O J D C C E N D S S L O A A L O Q L N S M V
A M H E R S V Y B I A T L M T J K P H I P A R
R M L S A P A T E Q S S E O B A P L E U Y G E
T U J T S S S R D B I I T R W I S O Z R L E L
H N N R H G T A F T L F N E O S E T P H A D E
Q I A U J R A W U M D O W T R I T M R U C D U
U T I C D I T R A M X B J K E J D O Z O O O R
A Y P T N D I A T S S H T F P G X L N V P N C
K S O I V D O E I R D C U Q E R R U R E A H B
E I T O M O N L D O O L F G N X Z A O O J F E
P Q S N B W A C T S U R V I V O R S T R B R P
T A Y G S N K U Y W P G E V O P G N Q E R I N
I C D G B X Z N L H C R O C S R V V Z Z P D Y
```

Find the following words in the puzzle.
Words are hidden ↑ ↓ → ← and ↘ .

APOCALYPSE
ARMAGEDDON
ASTEROID
BUG OUT
CATASTROPHE
COMMUNITY
CRASH
DESTRUCTION

DEVASTATION
DISASTER
DISINTEGRATE
DYSTOPIAN
EARTHQUAKE
ELE
ELECTROMAGNETIC
PULSE
FLOOD

GRID DOWN
HOPE
NUCLEAR WAR
RUIN
SCORCH
SHTF
SURVIVOR
TEOTWAWKI

YELLOWSTONE
ZOMBIE

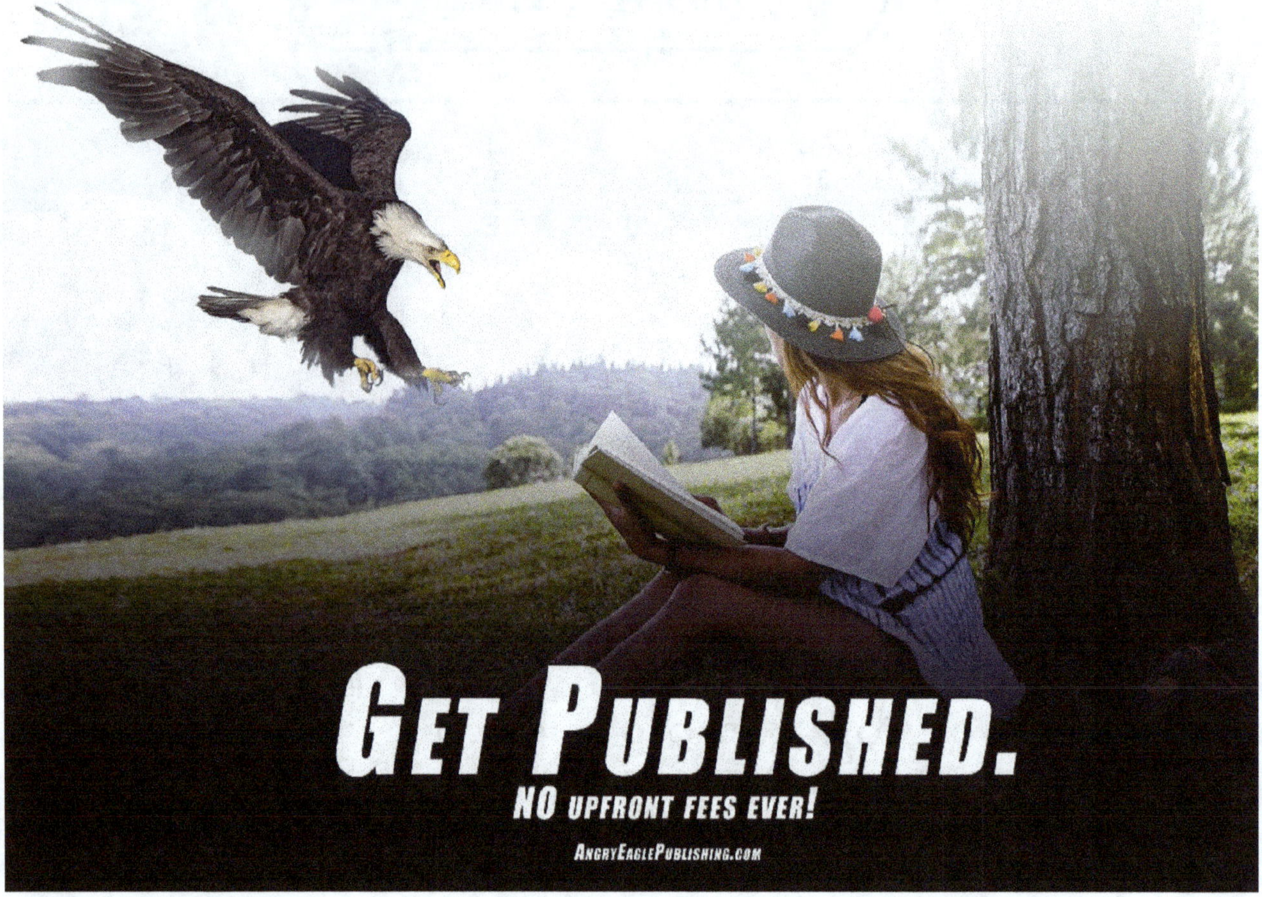
GET PUBLISHED.
NO UPFRONT FEES EVER!
AngryEaglePublishing.com

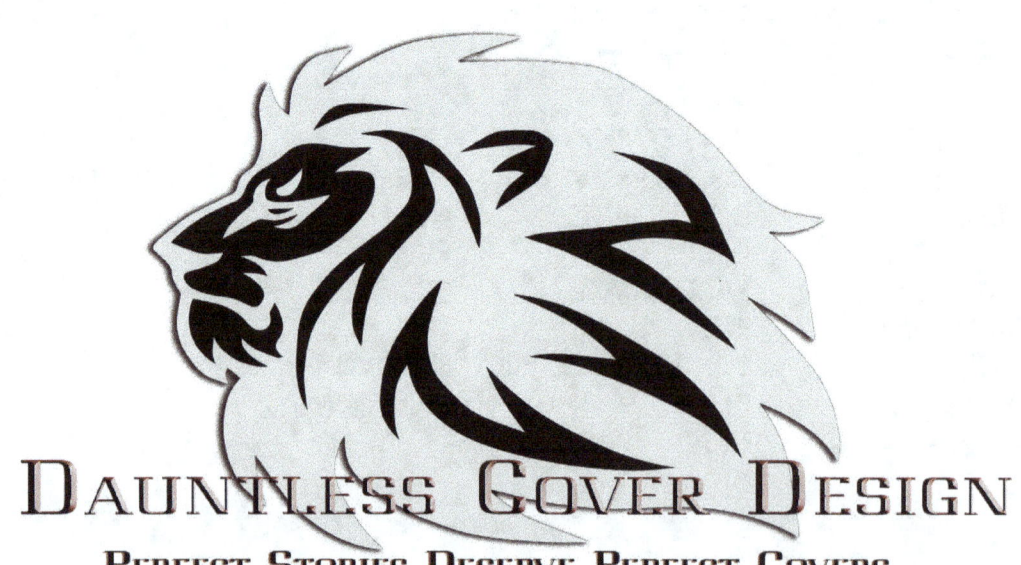

Individual Titles From Indie Authors — Nonfiction

Author Help
Your Book Won't Sell Itself
GJ Stevens

979-8392486045

$13.99 Paperback

$4.99 Kindle

https://www.amazon.com/dp/B0C2S59RSY

A helpful guide for authors, whether established or just starting out.

Despite writing and publishing eight novels, two novellas and an array of short stories over ten years, I still remember how daunting it was to start with a blank page.

Memoir
Coming Home
Naomi Kilbreth

978-1722112981

$15.74 Paperback

$5.99 Kindle

https://www.amazon.com/dp/B09882GDSM

Adventure is nothing new to the Kilbreth family, but what an adventure it is. A heart warming tale of one family's struggle to make it in the off grid world. An example for those who might like to go off grid and a warning to avoid some of the pitfalls. This don't miss book will bring you to tears, make you laugh, and make you think.

Herbal
Alison's Secret
N.A. Broadley

979-8820334900

$15.99 Paperback

$4.99 Kindle

https://www.amazon.com/dp/B09ZVC6GXJ

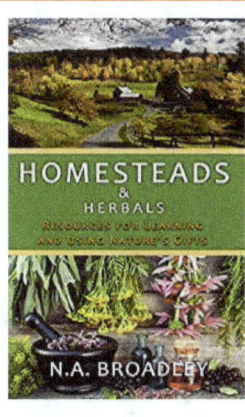

Discover some of the ways that herbals can come in handy on the homestead.

From the kitchen to the medicine cabinet these time honored remedies, brought to you in one place form a resource every home should not be without.

Humorous
Dammit Peckerhead
N.A. Broadley

978-1732621282

$8.89 Paperback

$3.99 Kindle

https://www.amazon.com/dp/1722112980

Allison has a secret. Like any farm wife, she is prepared for bad storms, bad times, and bad luck. But, even her husband is unaware that she is more prepared than the average farm wife.

Available on Amazon

Individual Titles From
Indie Authors—Anthologies

Zombie
Run From The Dead
Anthology

978-1736604380
$11.24 Paperback
$2.99 Kindle
https://www.amazon.com/dp/B09K6PYV2H

RUN! The Dead Walk An incredible journey through short stories offered by some of the finest writers in the Undead or Zombie genre, this book brings you fear, surprise, laughter, and a yearning for more with each story. Tales so cold they will make you shiver.

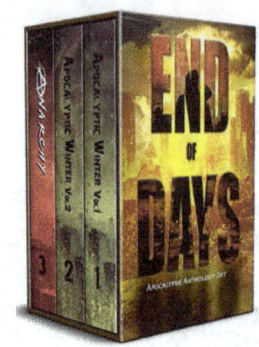

Post-Apocalyptic
End of Days
Boxed Anthology

$4.99 Kindle
https://www.amazon.com/dp/B0B4GJ6G32

kindle unlimited amazon

This book is smoking hot — Welcome to the Apocalypse! Enter stories by twenty authors where survivors must face the end of civilization as they know it, all while battling the brutal and deadly anarchy that is all too inevitable.

Zombie
Undead Worlds
Anthology

978-1626760288
$16.99 Paperback
$2.99 Kindle
https://www.amazon.com/dp/B07J599KFS

The fall of civilization! Zombies! Apocalypse!

The Reanimated Writers are back with their flagship anthology, Undead Worlds!

Dystopian
Broken Worlds
Anthology

978-0993657153
$11.49 Paperback
$2.99 Kindle
https://www.amazon.com/dp/B00Q7OD3H0

In a future of bleakness and roboticism, a totalitarian government enforces upon the people a lifestyle that lulls them into a state of obedience. Your career and social status are predestined and you cannot alter it - this is a reality that walks a fine line between evoking sensations of fear and inducing a sense of futility.

Individual Titles From Indie Authors—Scifi

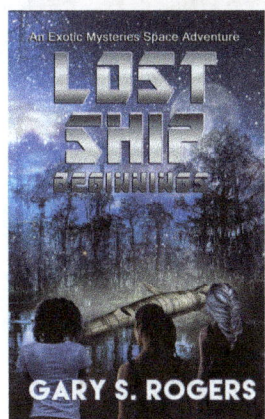

Exploration
Lost Ship
Gary S. Rogers

979-8986923130
$13.24 Paperback
$2.99 Kindle
https://www.amazon.com/dp/B0BRQVSSC9

The alien technology they found could change things for everyone. Dee, Takeeta, and Val want to do just that.

Space Opera
Echo Part One
M.L.Listen

979-8375963433
$17.50 Paperback
$2.99 Kindle
https://www.amazon.com/dp/B0BXBMBFVS

he year is 2377, and humanity has colonized the stars. The unstable division between the Unified Corporate Colonies and the Ursae Dynasty has fractured humanity into two distinct cultures that teeter on the brink of another galactic war.

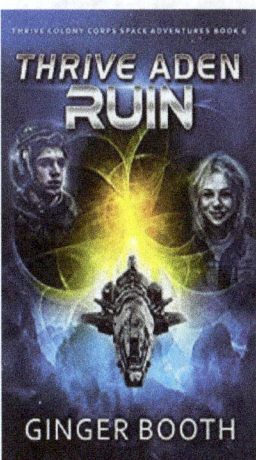

Colonization
Thrive Aden Run
Ginger Booth

979-8377068709
$18.24 Paperback
$5.99 Kindle
https://www.amazon.com/dp/B0BTH9TDKK

Sass and Ben foresee no major hurdles. They've succeeded at similar missions before. Then the Colony Corps abruptly loses them both.

Space Opera
Echo Part Two
M.L.Listen

978-1722112981
$17.85 Paperback
$2.99 Kindle
https://www.amazon.com/dp/B0BZM32PJW

As the crew embarks on a journey through an uncharted region of the universe, Kai will come to comprehend the depths of despair like never before. Kai will face a deeply disturbing situation that will push him to his limits and make him doubt his own mental stability.

Individual Titles From Indie Authors Zombie Titles

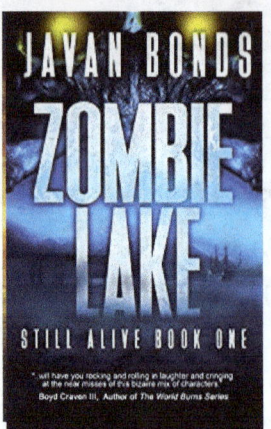

Zombie Humor
Zombie Lake
Javan Bonds

978-1542309202

$12.95 Paperback

$2.99 Kindle

https://www.amazon.com/dp/B01MY2S3A9

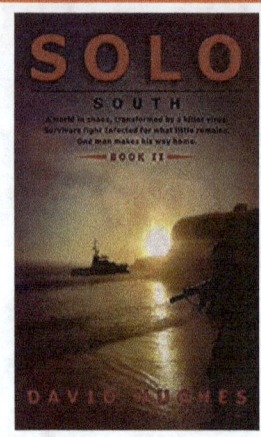

Zombie Adventure
SOLO: South
David Hughes

979-8373665216

$18.99 Paperback

$3.99 Kindle

https://www.amazon.com/dp/B0BVKVNGJD

Mo Collins, the reluctant Hero, has sailed around the country on board the replica pirate ship, the Viva Ancora and now he finds himself only miles from his childhood home. But now the world has gone to hell. Hordes of naked, blue, biting zombies have flooded the now dead Alabama lake town.

Off-the-grid and unaware. A descent into a surreal world. A non-stop fight to survive...

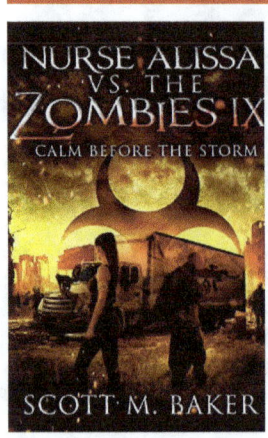

Zombie Horror
Nurse Alissa vs. the Zombies IX
Scott M. Baker

978-1736591598

$9.99 Paperback

$3.99 Kindle

https://www.amazon.com/dp/B0BYVBLKBW

Zombie Thriller
Stopping Power
GJ Stevens

979-8378563739

$15.99 Paperback

$5.99 Kindle

https://www.amazon.com/dp/B0C397TXHQ

Alissa and Chris survived the destruction of the underground nuclear storage bunker. Despite their injuries, they must escape and make their way home, a task easier said than done. Their journey will take them on a detour where Alissa's nursing skills will be put to good use.

After a gruelling training exercise in the Scottish mountains, Agent Carrie Harris is called to a place hidden from all civilisation. Ill-prepared and under-equipped, she discovers a secret world filled with gruesome evidence of events she can't comprehend.

Individual Titles From The Fall Series
Raventhorne Books

kindle unlimited amazon

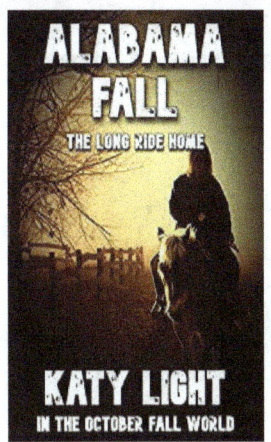

Post-Apocalyptic
Alabama Fall
Katy Light

$2.99 Kindle

https://www.amazon.com/dp/B0BW2X36RB

When stranded miles from their farm on the mountain with her two young children and two ponies after an EMP, a one-hour drive home by car turns into a dangerous major journey on horseback.

Available on Amazon

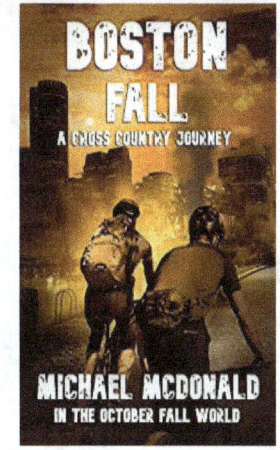

Post-Apocalyptic
Boston Fall
Michael McDonald

$2.99 Kindle

https://www.amazon.com/dp/B0C36GPXZK

*Christian Title

The story of a father and son, two thousand miles from home, trapped in an EMP nightmare!

Available on Amazon

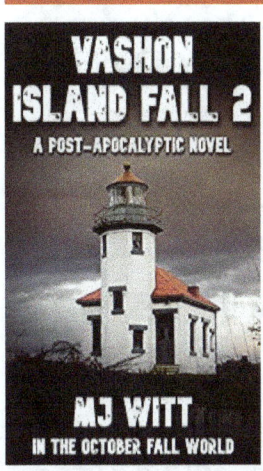

Post-Apocalyptic
Vashon Island Fall 2
MJ Witt

979-8375440583

$17.99 Paperback

$2.99 Kindle

https://www.amazon.com/dp/B0BSDN95W4

Amidst starvation, death, and the destruction of society, they are forced to deal with criminals turned pirates and raiders and a foreign army occupying their home under the guise of humanitarian aid.

Available on Amazon

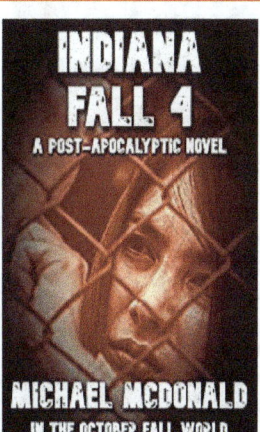

Post-Apocalyptic
Indiana Fall 4
Michael McDonald

979-8387603686

$12.99 Paperback

$2.99 Kindle

https://www.amazon.com/dp/B0BWSJHVVF

*Christian Title

The small community of Greensboro, Indiana, faces an unknown threat after an EMP attack on the United States several months earlier.

Available on Amazon

Individual Titles From
Indie Authors

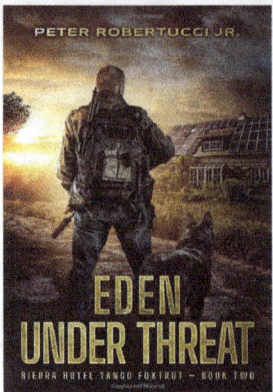

Post-Apocalyptic
Eden Under Threat
Pete Robertucci

978-1722112981

$15.99 Paperback

$5.99 Kindle

https://www.amazon.com/dp/B0BVC8LY93

When danger comes to his little slice of Eden, putting his wife Melissa and daughter Laykin in harm's way, he is forced to act. The mantra of Faith-Family-Country that he lived by is finally put to the test.

Post-Apocalyptic
The Darkness Grows
David Saylor

979-8393271084

$13.99 Paperback

$2.99 Kindle

https://www.amazon.com/dp/B0BZZKN1GH

Soon after the event, three wannabe dictators make a power grab for control of the isolated town, its residents, and its resources by imposing their idea of a local form of martial law, with some success.

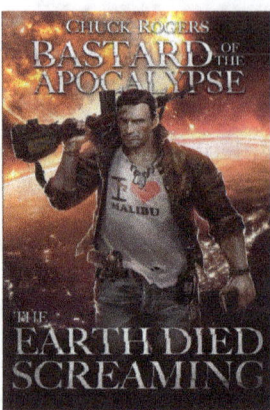

Post-Apocalyptic
Bastard of the Apocalypse
Chuck Rogers

978-1086050363

$14.99 Paperback

$5.99 Kindle

https://www.amazon.com/dp/B07VMVMBYY

Sometimes it takes a real bastard.My name is Benjamin Allen Frame.Last night the Earth died screaming.Today is Day One . . .

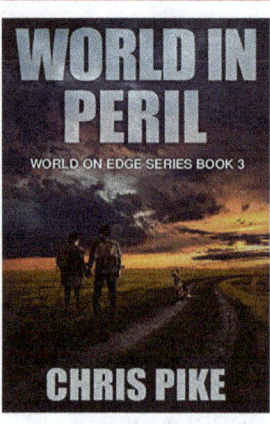

Post-Apocalyptic
World in Peril
Chris Pike

978-1722112981

$10.00 Paperback

$3.99 Kindle

https://www.amazon.com/dp/B0C2CZSV42

In World in Peril, loyalties will be tested, unexpected alliances will form, and traitors will resort to horrendous tactics to keep from being exposed. It's up to the survivors to serve justice.

Individual Titles From
Romance in the Apocalypse *spicy reads

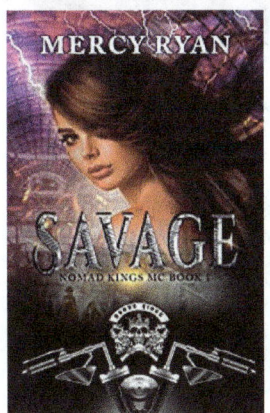

Zombie RH
Savage
Mercy Ryan

979-8985650228

$14.99 Paperback

$4.99 Kindle

https://www.amazon.com/dp/B09NT136PT

A world upside down where the dead roam free. They'll live on their own terms.

kindle unlimited amazon

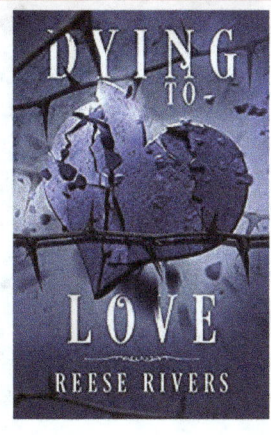

Zombie RH
Dying to Love
Reese Rivers

978-1989375129

$14.99 Paperback

$4.99 Kindle

https://www.amazon.com/dp/B095M74683

his isn't a blood and gore zombie novel. It's full of comedy, over protective men that just want to take care of her and a ton of sexy steam that happens behind a set of double fences.

Available on Amazon

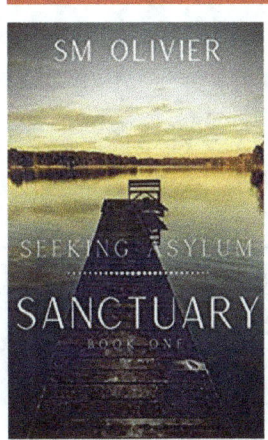

Zombie RH
Sanctuary:
Seeking Asylum Book 1
SM Oliver

$4.99 Kindle

https://www.amazon.com/dp/B087QNDLXF

Or so I thought. The news began to report disturbing stories about a new virus. This virus was turning people. The infected became violent and attacking anybody and everybody.

Dystopian
Stolen: Saving Setora
Raven Dark

Petra J. Knox

$2.99 Kindle

https://www.amazon.com/dp/B07BV5PVPY

It all began when the road warriors found me outside Hell's Burning, lost and dehydrated. When the bikers took me into The Compound, I thought I was saved.

Individual Titles From
Angry Eagle Publishing

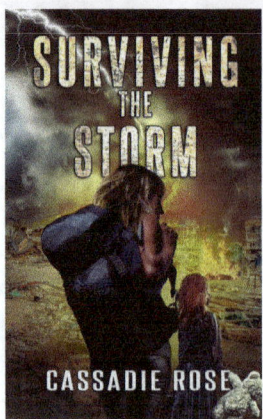

Post-Apocalyptic
Surviving the Storm
Cassadie Rose

979-8985650297

$12.99 Paperback

$4.99 Kindle

https://www.amazon.com/dp/B09XJ5WZL1

Can they survive the survivors of this? The situations that could cost them their lives? Determination, luck, and sheer will see them through.

Available on Amazon

Post-Apocalyptic
Sun's Fury
DJ Cooper

978-1732621244

$9.99 Paperback

$4.99 Kindle

https://www.amazon.com/dp/B07YDP17G4

Audiobook 1 Credit

The power is out. The question is... For how long. Quick thinking may save them, but death is right at the door. Jim and Ike begin to scavenge supplies as soon as they figure out just how bad the EMP Apocalypse could get.

Post-Apocalyptic
Altered Resonance
DJ Cooper

979-8986923123

$3.59 Paperback

$.99 Kindle

https://www.amazon.com/dp/B0BQ3Y44VV/

The accalimed short story from the Fractured World Anthology.

Have you ever wondered what kind of things microwave technology and 5G do to your brain?

Post-Apocalyptic
Invasion: Shadow Wars
A shared World

978-1736604366

$12.99 Paperback

$2.99 Kindle

https://www.amazon.com/dp/B09HR1LYRQ/

The whole city, perhaps even the world has gone crazy. An unlikely group of survivors; forced to work together, defend, and run, or risk losing their humanity.

Boxed Sets
Indie Authors

Kindle Unlimited — Amazon

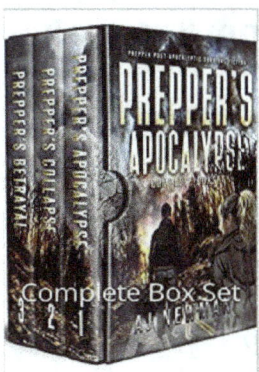

Post-Apocalyptic
Prepper's Apocalypse

AJ Newman

$5.99 Kindle

https://www.amazon.com/dp/B0B3S7JS6B

Audiobook 1 Credit

EMP blasts started the apocalypse during Tom and his family's return flight to San Francisco from Hawaii. Surviving the crash only caused them to confront the chaos of the apocalypse head-on.

Available on Amazon

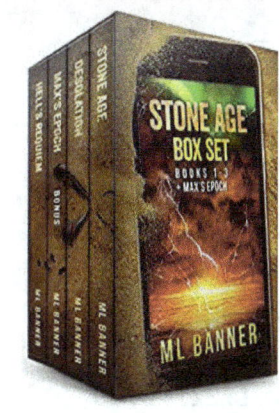

Post-Apocalyptic
Stone Age

M.L. Banner

$7.99 Kindle

https://www.amazon.com/dp/B085GKYQGY

The Thompson's must race to stay alive, while deciphering their part in a prophetic mystery, which may hold the key to their survival and that of humanity's.

Available on Amazon

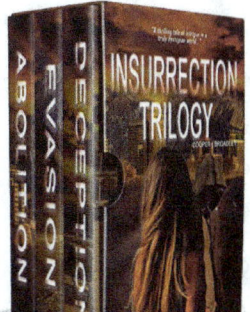

Dystopian
Insurrection Trilogy

DJ Cooper

N.A. Broadley

$6.99 Kindle

https://www.amazon.com/dp/B096L3Z6T7

Brother and sister, Kael and Zyla struggle against the harsh confines of their dystopian society. A life after the apocalypse, where servitude is second nature. Comply or face the Arena.

Available on Amazon

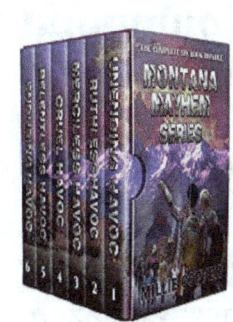

Post-Apocalyptic
Montana Mayhem

Millie Copper

$9.99 Kindle

https://www.amazon.com/dp/B0BKH6BXP5

When things don't work out as they hoped, will they become stranded in the wilderness? Or will each be able to find their way home?

Available on Amazon

Individual Titles From Indie Authors

kindle unlimited amazon

Post-Apocalyptic
Alison's Secret
D. Stalter

978-1722112981

$12.95 Paperback

$4.99 Kindle

https://www.amazon.com/dp/1722112980

Allison has a secret. Like any farm wife, she is prepared for bad storms, bad times, and bad luck. But, even her husband is unaware that she is more prepared than the average farm wife.

Available on Amazon

Post-Apocalyptic
Random Survival: The unit
Ray Wenck

978-1960545015

$12.99 Paperback

$3.99 Kindle

https://www.amazon.com/dp/1960545019

Weatherman and his team have discovered much about the cause of the pandemic that killed hundreds of millions of people but not enough about who released it.

Available on Amazon

Post-Apocalyptic
The Compound
B.J. Garcia

979-8376267349

$10.99 Paperback

$2.99 Kindle

https://www.amazon.com/dp/B0BXFYKV82

What would you do if the world as you knew it suddenly came crashing down around you?

A financial system in shambles, America slowly slips closer and closer toward collapse.

Available on Amazon

Post-Apocalyptic
The Last Day is Tomorrow
Abby Roze

979-8391104155

$7.44 Paperback

$2.99 Kindle

https://www.amazon.com/dp/B0C1J5P87P

Allison has a secret. Like any farm wife, she is prepared for bad storms, bad times, and bad luck. But, even her husband is unaware that she is more prepared than the average farm wife.

Available on Amazon

BOOK LISTINGS

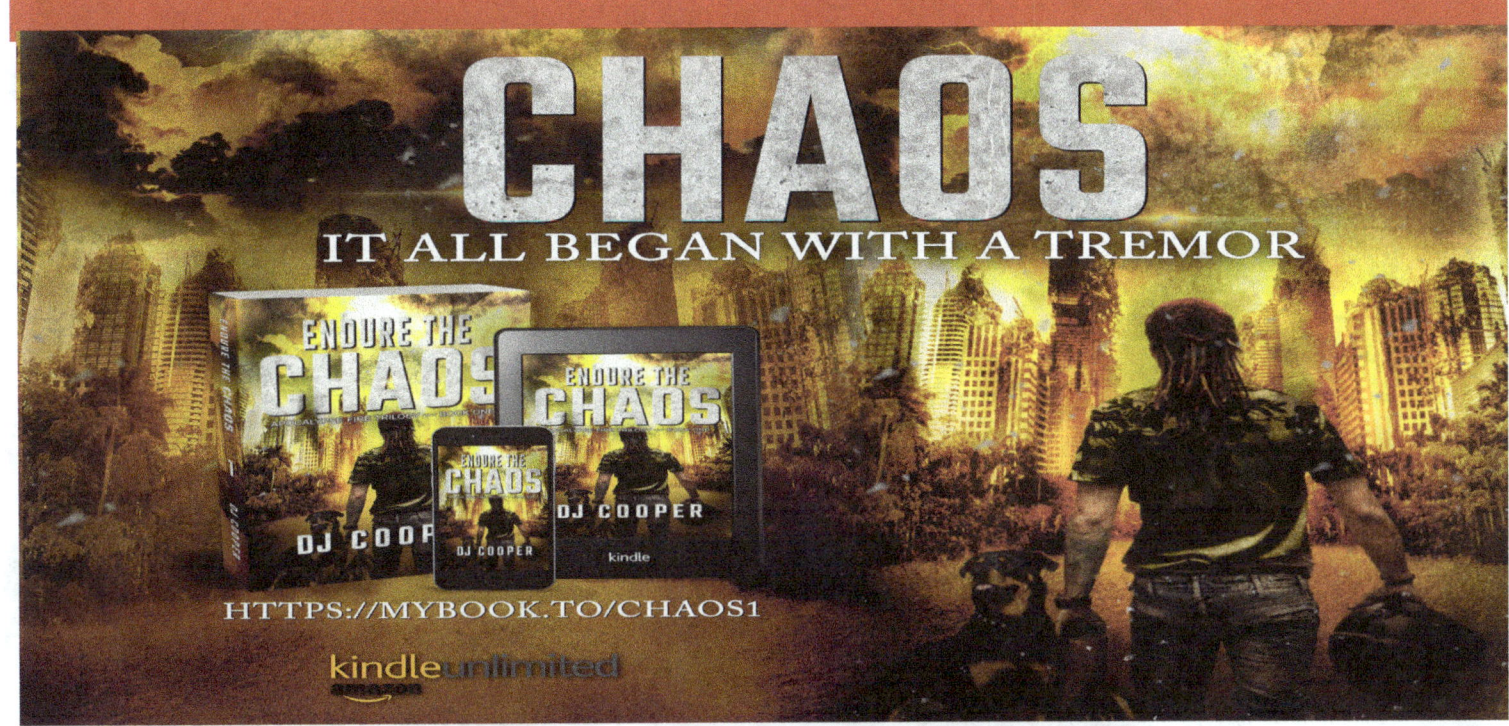

DJ COOPER

https://authoroftheapocalypse.com

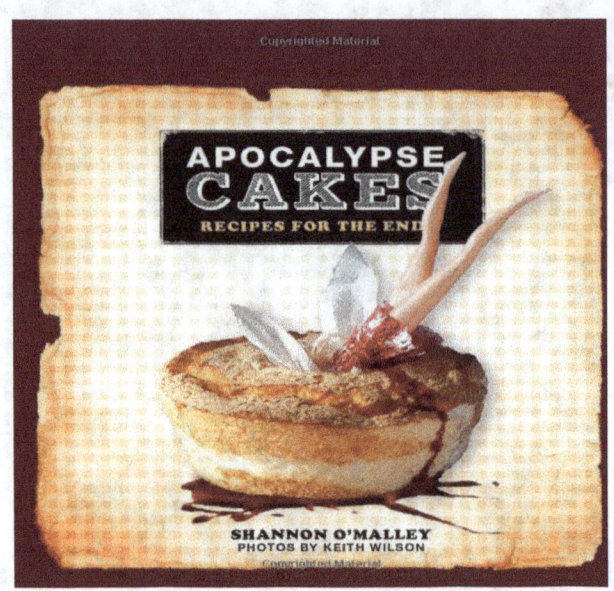

Get your apocalypse cooking groove on with this incredibly funny cookbook from Shannon O'Malley

https://www.amazon.com/dp/0762441062

EBOOK: $9.99
HARDCOVER $20.71
ISBN: 978-0762441068

Apocalyptic Fog

The result of this week's #DrinkYourGram where your votes helped shape this rendition of a classic Tiki Fog Cutter Cocktail.

- Difficulty: Intermediate

Servings	1 cocktail
Author	Monica C

🖨 Print

Ingredients

- 3/4 oz Aged Gin Crooked Oak's Barrel Reserve Gin
- 1/2 oz Blanco Tequila Tromba Tequila used here
- 1/2 oz Appleton's 8 yr Rum
- 1 oz Grapefruit Juice
- 3/4 oz Fresh Lime Juice
- 1/2 oz Orgeat Syrup
- 1 dash Angostura Bitters

Instructions

1. Fill your tiki glass with crushed ice.
2. Add all your ingredients, with a handful of cracked ice and give this a short shake.
3. Strain over crushed ice and garnish with mint leaves and grapefruit.

We discovered this one at https://www.liqculture.com/apocalyptic-fog/

END OF THE WORLD RECIPES

When reading about the end of the world what better thing than to have some snacks to go with it.

Zombie Intestines
[Sausage in Natural Casings]

Imagine the farmer harvesting a pig, the house is abuzz with the sound of the meat grinder being churned by a child while mom puts the chunks of meat and herbs in. The intestines have been cleaned and treated with salt brine. They will be hung to make part of the family stocks.

Ingredients

Hog Casings	Majoram
Pork Shoulder	Thyme
Coriander	Rosemary
Caraway	Salt

Making them
1. Grind up that meat.
2. Hands are great for mixing... Get the whole zombie thing going on and reach right into your ground meat and spice and give it a good mixing.
3. Be sure to squish it through your fingers for the best effect. Keep mixing, you gotta knead it almost like bread dough.
4. Best thing to do is get you a good sausage stuffer but we suppose maybe one of those injector things will do in a pinch.
5. Twist each segment tightly to separate the individual links.

Zombie Flesh
[Dehydrated Watermelon]

Wait... Watermellon is nearly all water, isn't that kind of counter intuitive? Watermelon has lots of great nutrients but check out that vitamin C. Along with some fiber, minerals, and sugars its a perfect snack for the road.

Ingredients
1 Watermelon and lots of time

Instructions
1. Cut watermelon and remove flesh from rind. Cut flesh into pieces as close to 1/4" thickness as you can. Remove seeds if possible.
2. Place on lined dehydrator trays and dehydrate at 135 degrees for ten forevers, or 18-24 hours, or until watermelon jerky is sufficiently dry and breaks when you bend it.
3. Store in airtight container.

ACRONYMS OF THE APOCALYPSE

Do you read books and find a bunch of letters and wonder what they mean in the books? Read on...

by DJ Cooper

Imagine if you will, TSHTF and TEOTWAWKI is on your doorstep. ROL is no longer, the LEOs are gone, and OPSEC is crucial to CYA. It is a GDE from a CME that produced a massive EMP. You are now thinking you won't be able to SIP and you might want to GOOD. You jump into the BOV to make a run for the BOL which is OTG. Getting ready to go, you grab the BOB which is a nice MOLLE setup that will incorporate the EDC; which alone might not cover it and you could have ended up SOL. With your MREs, you head out thinking to yourself, INCH. Hiding from MZBs because you know YOYO and you don't want to end up in someone's LOS. Hooking up with your MAG at the OP to set the SOP for COMMS with the CB or GMRS and to evaluate if there is any CBRN issues due to a CDC bulletin from the WHO over the EAS. Worried you might be FUBAR it is time to look at the ICE preps you've brought because this could mean your LTS. It is important to keep a PMA and at least you didn't forget the TP in case it all causes an uncontrolled BM when you realize you can't find your EOTWBFL. Hoping they didn't fall into the clutches of the GOLDEN HOARD it is time to ATL them while avoiding the POLLYANNA or SHEEPLE types JIC, because right now you DTA a

It's likely that some people could easily read and translate this paragraph. They are readily able to form the story and gain a whole scenario in this segment. But... what if you could not understand what was said here? This is often the issue with many (and not only those new to preparedness). It is a code or lingo that is used in the preparedness community and it would serve you well to know it. It is simple to find out what you don't know with these acronyms by googling it and adding "survival" to the search. Some of the terms highlighted in capital letters do not seem to be acronyms at all. Knowing what these also mean and will be important in the learning process. One of the hardest things for those new to the preparedness lifestyle is trying to understand these and other terms. With so much to assimilate and consider, just the logistics of preparedness can be overwhelming; add to it the understanding of events and scenarios and the psychology surrounding it all and you have information overload. The conversation shouldn't be difficult and needs to be easily understood, but unfortunately it often isn't, which adds to confusion and frustration. Think about this for a moment. Post SHTF and you receive a bit of INTEL about some MZBs are closing on your LP... What do you do? If you don't know what the message is telling you, WTSHTF there will be no Google to translate. So, learn these, take a little time to make a list and remember it is important to be BSTS.

CHECK OUT THE BOOK ASYLUM PODCAST

WITH JACK CHILDRESS

AUTHOR INTERVIEWS | BOOK REVIEWS
AND SO MUCH MORE...
JOIN THE FUN!

https://www.youtube.com/channel/UCUHjU3S-FKJ2KiKhKo-4PxAw

Get in on the fun and laughs with this bunch of zombie freaks.

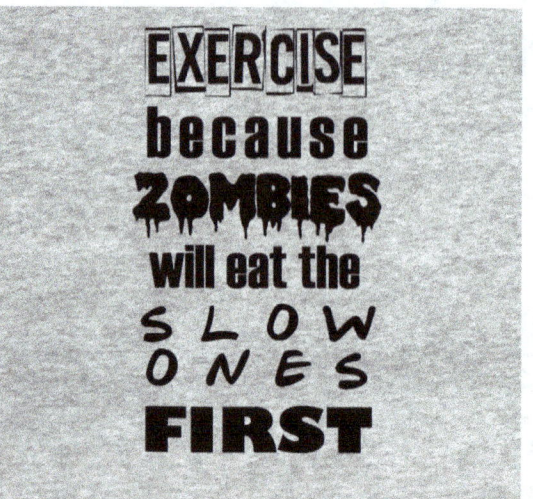

Join in the antics

HEAD OVER TO THE FACEBOOK GROUP TODAY!

- BIRTHDAY FUN
- GIVEAWAYS
- BOOKS
- AUTHORS
- FUNNY CHATS
- VIDEOS
- DISCUSSIONS

Come on in and sit a while, the authors came to chat all things zombie

ZOMPOC INVASION

Amazing wordsmiths that bring you anything from laughs to tears in the zombie genre. Check them out!

MEET THE AUTHORS OF THE UNDEAD

- JAVAN BONDS
- JS PATRICK
- AL WHITE
- COURTNEY KONSTANTIN
- GJ STEVENS
- MIKE ROBBINS
- NIC ROADS
- ANGEL RAMON
- S P OLDHAM
- BEN BLACK
- CAL BRETT
- RHIANNON FRATER
- MATT HAY
- D KAY FRASER
- ALATHIA MORGAN
- DAVID MOODY
- CHRIS PHILBROOK
- CA HOAKS
- RICHARD R ROSE
- RICKY FLEET

Thrive Gandhi Requiem

Discover high-tech prizes, and horrors, in the series finale!
Tripping through terrifying futures, Ben Acosta strives to regain his home universe and timeline. But is he truly the one piloting his lost starship? Or does someone else have an agenda?
lutionize the League! But their social mores combine the worst of all worlds, subjugating women and lower castes.

$5.99 e-book price on Amazon
https://www.amazon.com/dp/B0C39G8P43

Slow Collapse 2: Control

Devastated and broken, America finds new ways to reach ultimate lows. Terrorist attacks continue to kill Americans inside their owns shores, while confusion dominates the globe. While an old enemy finds new ways to cripple America, financial institutions worldwide are going bankrupt, and economies tank.

$4.99 e-book price on Amazon
https://www.amazon.com/dp/B0C39BK4XT

Wild-Eyed Southern Boyz: Dead Cold War

Over a year has passed since The Uprising, and the Smoky Mountains are slowly healing from the zombie outbreak that threatened the entire world. Buford and Rue begin their new lives protecting their beloved home, while Buford balances his duties between being a park ranger and training a new generation of Red Tunic initiates.

$2.99 e-book price on Amazon
https://www.amazon.com/dp/B0C448ZR4R

Thrive Gandhi Requiem by **Ginger Booth**

Slow Collapse 2: Control by **S.M. Little**

Wild-Eyed Southern Boyz: Dead Cold War by **Richard R. Rose**

"There's a gas station up ahead." stated Bob. "I'm almost out of hours of service, so that may be a good place to let you take over driving."

Sheila sighed, "That sounds good. I wouldn't mind going in and hitting the soda fountain. That greasy burger hasn't been sitting in my stomach very well. Maybe a soft drink will make me feel better."

"Yeah, that does sound good." stated Bob, as he noticed the state police cars blocking the oncoming lane. He easily wheeled the semi-truck into the gas station, and parked it away from the pumps. Both he and Sheila exited the cab, and headed into the gas station.

Sam wheeled his Harley into the gas station, as the engine started sputtering. Ralph followed closely. "Let's fuel up the bikes, and then I could use something cold to drink." he stated, as he glanced towards the building. "Hey, there's that babe again. Damn, she sure is cute."

"Just pump the fuel, Sam." growled Ralph. "I want to get out of here as quickly as we can. Those cops are set up out on the road, but I think we can take the back way out and miss them."

"Ok, but I'm going in and hit the soda fountain. I'm almost as thirsty as my bike." laughed Sam, as he started pumping 91-Octane gasoline into the Harley's gas tank.

Ralph followed suit.

Sheila pulled open the door to the dingy white-brick gas station, and was assaulted by the overly loud music, playing The Animals song "We've Gotta Get Out of This Place".

"I haven't heard that song in a long time." stated Bob. "But, it's strangely appropriate."

Sheila laughed, and then belched loudly, as she headed toward the soda fountain. "Out of order?" she shouted much too loudly. "Damn it. Well, I'll just grab a six pack of bottled soda then." she stated, as she grabbed a six pack of Coke Zero bottles.

"Uh, Sheila, we need to get out of here now." exclaimed Bob in a whisper.

Sheila turned and saw a disheveled clerk as he was trying to climb over the counter to reach them. Something was obviously seriously wrong with him. Perhaps it was his grayish-yellow skin, or the fact that he had blood leaking from his eye sockets. Or, it could have been the cut across his chest, which exposed his rib bones.

Sheila quick-stepped around the end of an aisle, and headed toward the door, just as Sam and Ralph came in.

"Hey, darlin', are you leaving so soon?" asked Sam, as he turned to face Sheila.

At that moment, the clerk reached across the counter, and grabbed the collar of Sam's leather jacket, which allowed the clerk to scrape his body across the counter.

"Aieeee!" screamed Sam, and he struggled to get out of his leather jacket. "Get it off me! Get it off!" screamed Sam.

Ralph jumped to Sam's aid, and started hitting the clerk with a conveniently positioned case of light beer. Sheila and Bob took advantage of the diversion to slip out the door, as they ran for their truck. It only took them a few moments to climb in the truck, start it up, and to accelerate out of the parking lot, taking part of the sign with them.

Sam and Ralph weren't so lucky, in that the altercation attracted the attention of the burger bar clerk, who staggered over, in a most dead-like manner, to join in the festivities. Sam finally extracted himself from his leather jacket, and sacrificed it, as he and Bob escaped out the door of the gas station.

***

"Damn! That was scary." exclaimed Sheila, as she shifted gears in the semi-tractor. "I don't ever want to encounter any of those things again!"

"Agreed." replied Bob.

"I don't know about you, but I think our destination just changed. Do you think the company would be upset if we went from Atlanta to Los Angeles, via Alaska?" asked Sheila.

The End...

And, I damn sure don't like the idea of just sitting here. So, I guess we'll follow them. Besides, we need fuel. I'm really beginning to wish we'd never taken this job, though." stated Ralph.

"Yeah, but we have three hundred thousand reasons why I'm glad we took this job." smiled Sam. "Now, let's get out of here."

"Watch out!" yelled Ralph. "It's that damned truck again!"

Sam jammed on the brakes on his bike, and slid to a stop just inches from the roadway, as the semi-truck came barreling past, again splashing water all over both bikers. "You mother..." stuttered Sam, as he gave a one-finger salute to the truck.

Sergeant Murphy's voice came over Officer Denton's radio, "There's a gas station a little ways in front of us. Looks like they still have electricity. We'll establish a perimeter there, and stop any traffic from going into the affected area."

Officer Denton keyed his radio, "What about people coming out of the area? Do we stop them?".

"No, let them through. The only ones we've seen have been that truck and those bikers, but they may be gone by now." replied Murphy.

"Do we know how this thing is spread? Is it through physical contact, or via bites, or some other means?" asked Denton.

"I don't know. They've sent some doctors in to study the affected people, but the last I've heard is that they've all been attacked and killed. So, they're running short of medical personnel, especially after that outbreak at the hospital." explained Murphy.

"Gosh, I wish we knew. I'm not even sure how to protect ourselves." stated Denton, with a worried twitch in his voice.

"There's a gas station up ahead." stated Bob. "I'm almost out of hours of service, so that may be a good place to let you take over driving."

Sheila sighed, "That sounds good. I wouldn't mind going in and hitting the soda fountain. That greasy burger hasn't been sitting in my stomach very well. Maybe a soft drink will make me feel better."

"Yeah, that does sound good." stated Bob, as he noticed the state police cars blocking the oncoming lane. He easily wheeled the semi-truck into the gas station, and parked it away from the pumps. Both he and Sheila exited the cab, and headed into the gas station.

Sam wheeled his Harley into the gas station, as the engine started sputtering. Ralph followed closely. "Let's fuel up the bikes, and then I could use something cold to drink." he stated, as he glanced towards the building. "Hey, there's that babe again. Damn, she sure is cute."

"Just pump the fuel, Sam." growled Ralph. "I want to get out of here as quickly as we can. Those cops are set up out on the road, but I think we can take the back way out and miss them."

"Ok, but I'm going in and hit the soda fountain. I'm almost as thirsty as my bike." laughed Sam, as he started pumping 91-Octane gasoline into the Harley's gas tank.

Ralph followed suit.

Sheila pulled open the door to the dingy white-brick gas station, and was assaulted by the overly loud music, playing The Animals song "We've Gotta Get Out of This Place".

"I haven't heard that song in a long time." stated Bob. "But, it's strangely appropriate."

Sheila laughed, and then belched loudly, as she headed toward the soda fountain. "Out of order?" she shouted much too loudly. "Damn it. Well, I'll just grab a six pack of bottled soda then." she stated, as she grabbed a six pack of Coke Zero bottles.

"Uh, Sheila, we need to get out of here now." exclaimed Bob in a whisper.

Sheila turned

"I don't know. They've sent some doctors in to study the affected people, but the last I've heard is that they've all been attacked and killed. So, they're running short of medical personnel, especially after that outbreak at the hospital." explained Murphy.

"Gosh, I wish we knew. I'm not even sure how to protect ourselves." stated Denton, with a worried twitch in his voice.

"You ditched all of that liquid, didn't you?" asked Ralph nervously, yelling to make himself heard over the two powerful motorcycle engines.

Bob mashed his steel-toed leather boot down harder on the accelerator pedal, and watched as both the tachometer and speedometer increased.

"Crap! It's the fuzz!" screamed Sam, as he glanced behind himself, at the two rapidly approaching police cruisers, both with their lights flashing, and their sirens bleating loudly.

"You ditched all of that liquid, didn't you?" asked Ralph nervously, yelling to make himself heard over the two powerful motorcycle engines.

"Yeah, I got rid of all of it. But, we have all that money in our saddle bags. Should we ditch it?" asked Sam.

"Oh, hell no!" screamed Ralph. "Let's see if we can outrun them."

Both Sam and Ralph cranked on the throttles to their motorcycles, and the powerful Harleys responded by leaping ahead, throwing massive rooster-tails of water in their wake.

"Remember that I'm low on fuel." screamed Sam.

"Yeah, I know. But, there's that damned semi ahead of us. Let's see if we can get around him, and maybe we can lose the fuzz." cried Ralph.

Both bikers performed a dangerous passing maneuver, on the rain slicked road, across a double yellow line, while going around a curve. Luck was with them, as they completed the pass, and pulled rapidly away from the semi-truck.

"Damned bikers!" screamed Bob, as the two motorcyclists made an unsafe passing maneuver around his truck. "Must be them that the cops are chasing."

"Um, I don't know." replied Sheila, as she glanced in the rear-view mirror. "They seem intent on following us. Maybe you'd better stop."

Bob eased off of the accelerator, and searched for a wide place along the side of the road where he could bring the semi to a safe stop. He finally found a wide pull-off, where he eased the semi onto the gravel, and brought it to a stop. One of the state police cars pulled along side him, and the officer stepped out. "Don't stop. Keep going, as far and as fast as you can. There's some serious stuff going on around here, and, trust me, you want no part of it." With that, the officer stepped back into the cruiser, and sped off, followed closely by the other police cruiser.

"Whew, that was close." whispered Sam, who was perched on his Harley, which was parked behind some trees, off the road.

"Yeah, really." agreed Ralph, as he watched the two police cruisers fly past them, their lights and sirens still operating.

"So, what do we do?" asked Sam. "Do we pull out and follow them, or do we sit here for a while, or do we turn back and go the other way?"

"Damn, I don't know. I'm not anxious to be following the fuzz. But, I don't want to go back where we came from.

"I'm not too fond of the idea of turning into one of those things either." replied Bob, as he reached over with his right hand, and held Sheila's left hand. "I'll promise you this; I'll do everything in my power to protect you. How's that?"

"Oh, Bob." sobbed Sheila. "I think I love you."

Bob laughed. "I've loved you for years. But, let's get the hell out of here, while we still can." continued Bob, as he mashed his foot down on the accelerator, and the large Cummins Diesel engine growled.

"Hey, Ralph, here comes someone." yelled Sam, from the edge of the road. "See if you can flag them down. Maybe they'll let us siphon a gallon of gasoline."

Ralph snarled, "I can't believe you ran out of gas. Why didn't you fill your bike up at one of the fuel stations we stopped at, while dropping off the product?"

Sam glared at Ralph. "Because I didn't know we'd be running for our lives. Now, flag this vehicle down."

"What the hell?" yelled Bob, as he laid on the air-horn, and switched to the wrong lane, to pass the two guys on the side of the road standing beside motorcycles.

"It's those idiot bikers." laughed Sheila. "Looks like you really gave them a bath, too, with the way you splashed them."

"Fools!" exclaimed Bob, and he continued down the highway in the truck.

***

"Damn it!" yelled Sam, as he tried to wipe some of the water off of himself. "It was that butt-hole truck driver we keep running into. And, he didn't stop!"

Ralph snarled out a laugh. "Did you really expect him to? Besides, it wouldn't have helped. That was a Diesel truck, and our bikes use gasoline."

Sam kicked a rock which was laying on the side of the road out of frustration, and then hopped clumsily as pain shot up his leg. "Ow! Hey, what about if I siphon a quart of gasoline out of your bike? That'll give me enough to get to the next fuel station?"

"Ok, but hurry up." instructed Ralph, as he waited for Sam to perform the siphoning procedure.

***

"Denton, orders are to fall back. We're being overrun." commanded Sergeant Murphy.

Officer Denton pushed and shoved his way past several of the creatures, narrowly avoiding some open jaws, before he quickly jumped in his cruiser, slamming the door solidly. He started the cruiser, and used it to push a half dozen of the creatures out of his way, as he fled the area. Denton headed north on highway 27, until he reached the intersection with highway 48, where he turned to the west. He sighed in relief as he noticed Sergeant Murphy's bloodied cruiser closely following him.

***

"Drat! We've got cops following us." exclaimed Bob, as he stared into the rear-view mirror.

"Ignore them." commanded Sheila. "Put the pedal to the metal, and let's get out of here. Besides, they can't be chasing us. We haven't done anything wrong."

Bob mashed his steel-toed leather boot down harder on the accelerator pedal, and watched as both the tachometer and speedometer increased.

"Crap! It's the fuzz!" screamed Sam, as he glanced behind himself, at the two rapidly approaching police cruisers, both with their lights flashing, and their sirens bleating loudly.

"There are just so many of them." stated Denton. "It's almost like the whole town has been affected, and that they're all heading this way. Maybe it's our flashing lights and siren that's attracting them?"

"Well, we can't very well turn them off, or people will crash into us." explained Murphy. "Just do what you can to divert traffic from getting on the interstate, and try to stay away from them."

***

Bob continued driving the semi-truck, as Sheila sat in the passenger seat, and alternated between tuning the truck's radio and the CB radio. "Bob, I'm scared. These reports we're hearing indicate something's seriously wrong out there."

Bob nodded glumly, as he glanced over at Sheila, who was wearing a pair of tight-fitting jeans, with a red and blue plaid shirt, which was a size too small for her. "If I didn't have this load behind me, I'd be heading away from here as fast as this truck would take us. But, we've got to deliver this stuff, before it goes bad."

"I know." sighed Sheila heavily. "It just looks like we're heading into the heart of the problem."

"Look at that!" exclaimed Bob, as he pointed to a fireball off in the distance to his left, and well ahead of them. "That didn't look very good at all."

"Might have been over on the interstate." explained Sheila. "Maybe we ought to stay on highway 48 for a bit, rather than taking highway 27 to the south. It seems like all of the trouble is centered around the interstate highway."

Bob nodded. "Yeah, you have a point. Let's stick to highway 48 for a while. We've got a full load of fuel, which ought to take us close to a thousand miles. Aww, this isn't good." added Bob, as he noticed a set of darkened traffic lights ahead. "We're coming up on the junction of highways 48 and 27, and it looks like the electricity is out. What do you think, Sheila? Go south on 27 back toward the interstate, go west on 48, or go north on 27?"

Sheila looked at the satellite navigation map, as Bob slowed the truck for the intersection. "South to the interstate is no good. North on 27 takes us into the mountains, and I'd just as soon not take this rig into the mountains. So, let's stay on 48 going west. Hey, what's that on the sign?" asked Sheila, as she pointed to a green road sign, with something dark gray and red laying over the top of it.

"Looks like a sock, and a bloody sock at that." explained Bob, as he pressed down on the accelerator, and sped through the darkened intersection without stopping."

"Bob!" exclaimed Sheila. "You were supposed to stop for a darkened traffic light."

"You didn't see him?" asked Bob in a wavering voice. "The guy off to our left, with the blood spurting out of a hole in his neck."

"What?" screamed Sheila. "You mean the reports on the radio were true? We're really facing zombies?"

"I don't know if he was a zombie or not, but he sure looked like one. And, I just didn't want to get bloody hand-prints on the side of our truck, so I didn't stop." explained Bob.

"Bob, I'm really scared now." cried Sheila. "I mean, well, I'm not afraid of dying, but I don't want to turn into one of those things. It's not like I have anything to live for. My parents are both dead, and I don't have any aunts or uncles. My ex-husbands are all idiots, and I've never had any children, never wanted any, really. But, those things terrify me worse than dying." continued Sheila, as tears ran down her face.

"No, no. She volunteered the information. Said it was too late for anyone to stop her now. Something about she was going to pump that blue liquid into the water system, and contaminate it. It's something called Elixir of Zombies, or something like that." continued Sam.

"Damn it. Shut up. I don't want to know. Now, let's get out of here." commanded Ralph, as he shifted his motorcycle into gear, and eased out of the parking area, and toward the road.

***

"It's those damned bikers again." yelled Bob, as he pulled the cord for the air horn. "I'd run their asses over, if I wasn't afraid it'd scratch the truck."

Sheila laughed nervously, as she watched the truck fly past the tiny gas station, with the bikers positioned near the highway. "Getting a bit aggressive, aren't you? That's no way for a Knight of the Road to be talking."

Bob looked sheepish. "Sorry. Maybe it's about time I let you take over. My hours of service are about up anyway, and I must be getting tired if I'm allowing stupid people to upset me."

"Oh, don't apologize." purred Sheila. "It's just that I've never seen you like this before, and, well, umm, I kind of like it."

Bob glanced at her suspiciously.

"Well, maybe it was all of the talk of motorcycles and big throbbing things between my legs, but a gal has needs." continued Sheila. "Maybe we should both take a break at the next truck-stop. and test out the suspension on this big rig. I mean, we've been driving together for what, five years now, and well, I'm kind of developing feelings for you."

Bob smiled. He'd had a crush on Sheila since the first run they had made together. But, he had conducted himself in a professional manner. Plus, Sheila had explained how she had three failed marriages behind her, and had sworn off of guys. He was just glad to have been paired up with a talented driver, one he could trust with the truck, while he was sleeping in the sleeper. But, the idea of a romantic interest from Sheila was even better.

***

"Sarge, I don't know what's going on." exclaimed Officer Denton. "These people are getting run over, having their legs broken, their arms crushed, and their guts blown out all of the road, and they're still alive, or, at least, I think they're alive. They're still moving. Not only that, but they continue attacking people. It's almost like they're, no, I shouldn't say it, but I'm going to anyway, zombies."

"Now, Denton, you know that there are no such things as zombies." corrected Sergeant Murphy.

"Well, I know that, Sarge, but I don't know how else to explain what's happening. Normal people don't crawl away from being run over by a semi. But, that's what these, um, things are doing. And, they're attacking and biting people." continued Denton.

"It's just that they're on some good drugs, some very good drugs." stated Murphy, as he watched one of the creatures, which was wearing blue denim coveralls, throw itself in front of an ambulance, only to be crushed, before crawling after the ambulance.

"I'm pretty sure it's more than just drugs." stated Denton, with a worried look in his blue eyes.

"Well, we'll do what we can to stop traffic. We'll just have to hope that the medical personnel can deal with all of them." replied Murphy, as he watched one of the ambulances overturn, after hitting a tall, blonde creature, which was wearing a short red dress.

Bob jammed on the air-brakes, and held tightly to the steering wheel, as two motorcycles flew past him, in the passing lane, and then pulled back into his lane, much too close for comfort. "Damned bikers!" he yelled, as he fought to control the truck. "Do they have a suicide wish or something? You simply don't change lanes in front of an 80,000 pound truck, and live to tell about it!"

"Sorry about that." laughed Sheila, as she wiped up the errant pieces of food which had flown from her mouth. "I was trying to yell 'Watch out', but, well, you got the gist of it. Ah, but to be young and foolish again, with something big and powerful throbbing between my legs."

Bob coughed. "I thought you'd sworn off of guys?"

"I meant a motorcycle." explained Sheila, as she blushed. "I used to ride one, ages ago, but I haven't been on one in years. Still, I occasionally get the urge to climb back on one, and go flying carefree down the highway, with the breeze on my knees, and the air in my hair. Of course, I sometimes get the urge to climb on top of a guy, too. But, I'm afraid that I'm old enough and wise enough to know better than to do either of those things now."

Bob nodded wisely. "I'm afraid I'm too old to be doing that."

"What? Riding a motorcycle or a gal?" giggled Sheila.

Bob chuckled, "I meant a motorcycle. I'll never be too old to ride a gal, at least if I could ever find the right one. But, I'm not sure there's one out there for me. Meanwhile, I seem to spend all of my time stuck in the cab of a truck. It's not like I get to attend ice cream socials or things like that."

Sheila sighed heavily.

***

"Hot damn!" exclaimed Sam, as he handed over the bottles of blue liquid he'd been carrying around, and received a brown paper bag stuffed with cash. "Enjoy your product." he laughed, as he winked at the middle-aged fat lady he had received the cash from.

"Oh, I will!" the fat lady laughed evilly, as she watched Sam walk out of the gas station's bathroom.

Sam stashed the cash in the saddle bags of his Harley, before he mounted the bike. He nodded quickly to Ralph, as he started the Harley. "Let's get far away from this place."

"Hot damn!" exclaimed Sam, as he handed over the bottles of blue liquid he'd been carrying around, and received a brown paper bag stuffed with cash. "Enjoy your product." he laughed, as he winked at the middle-aged fat lady he had received the cash from.

"Oh, I will!" the fat lady laughed evilly, as she watched Sam walk out of the gas station's bathroom.

Sam stashed the cash in the saddle bags of his Harley, before he mounted the bike. He nodded quickly to Ralph, as he started the Harley. "Let's get far away from this place."

Ralph smiled, from under his white helmet. "I like the way you think", he replied, as he started his own Harley.

"No, I mean, seriously. That gal back there said that, if we wanted to live, we need to get as far away from this place as we can. I'm thinking Mexico, or maybe South America." explained Sam.

"You been asking questions again, haven't you? I told you about that!" exclaimed Ralph, as he looked suspiciously over at Sam.

"No, no. She volunteered the information. Said it was too late for anyone to stop her now. Something about she was going to pump that blue liquid into the water system, and contaminate it. It's something called Elixir of Zombies, or something like that." continued Sam.

Sheila nodded. "Let's do it." she replied, as another police car, with its blue lights flashing ominously, sped past the truck-stop., and established a roadblock on the interstate highway, near the exit they had just used.

"Yeah, let's get out of here before they block the secondary roads, too." continued Bob, as he started up the truck, and shifted it into gear.

***

"Did you see that babe that got in that truck?" asked Sam, as he looked at Ralph, who was reclining lazily on his Harley-Davidson motorcycle.

"Huh? What? Babe? Naw, I didn't see anything. I dozed off, man." Ralph relied, as he lifted the dark visor of his helmet. "It was probably just your typical lot-lizard."

"No, I don't think so. She was a major cutie. Looked to be higher class than your typical lot-lizard." explained Sam, as he climbed aboard his own Harley motorcycle.

"Is that all you ever think about?" asked Ralph rhetorically. "Forget about the babes. Did you make the delivery?"

"No. He didn't show." explained Sam.

"Crap! You mean you still have the stuff on you?" asked Ralph, with a worried look in his eyes.

Sam scowled, and spit on the ground between their two motorcycles, "What was I supposed to do? Leave a hundred thousand worth of product sitting on a table, where some brat could run away with it?

I'm not letting loose of this stuff until we get our money."

"Well, at least we got the bucks for that last batch we dropped off in the town we just came from." explained Ralph, as he gestured lazily towards the west with his right hand. "And, that hundred K will take us a long way".

"I know, but 200 K would be better than 100 K. Plus, I don't like hauling this stuff around with me. I damned sure don't want to get stopped by the fuzz with this stuff, and there sure are a lot of them flying around with their lights on tonight." added Sam. "Besides, do we even know what this stuff is? I mean, I know it's not Heroin, Fentanyl, or Coke, but there's got to be something magical about it if people are willing to pay us so much just to transport it."

"Damn it, Sam. You know better than to ask questions like that. Asking questions like that will get us killed. Now, shut your mouth, and let's head to the next delivery site. Maybe they'll take the rest of the stuff, and we can be done with this." stated Ralph, as a bead of sweat rolled down between his brown eyes.

"Yeah, you're right." agreed Sam. "Let's get the hell out of here. Which way to the next delivery site?"

Ralph stood his Harley up, and retracted the kickstand, as he thumbed the electric starter. "North, up highway 23. The delivery point is a little gas station near the intersection of highway 48."

Sam started his Harley, and the two bikers pulled out, leaving only a cloud of dust behind, as they sped north on highway 23.

***

"matmp ompth!" yelled Sheila, through a mouthful of greasy burger, which caused bits of onion and tomato to fly from her mouth.

He quickly grabbed the receipt the pump spit out, before he walked to the other side, and tapped his foot anxiously as he waited for that tank to fill, and for the nozzle to shut off. Finally, the right-side nozzle clicked off, and he repeated the procedure of hanging up the green Diesel fuel nozzle, replacing the cap on his fuel tank, and grabbing the second receipt.

Uncharacteristically, Bob jammed the receipts in his pocket, unwilling to take the time to read the amounts. He charged into the truck-stop., bypassing a lonely dog which was begging for food near the front door, and noticed that the counter was empty, which he found unusual. Glancing around the building, he spotted Sheila walking toward him with a bag of burgers, with the grease already soaking through the brown paper of the bag. "Did you see the clerk?" asked Bob curiously.

"No. Only person I saw was the kid working the burger bar, and he looked real nervous. I asked him if he knew anything about why the highway was closed, and he just shrugged. Didn't look too bright, if you know what I mean." explained Sheila.

"Damn!" cursed Bob. "Let me go drain the dragon real quick, and I'll join you back in the truck. I've got another couple of hours of service left, so I'll keep driving. But, see what you can find out on the radio, or on the CB. Might even check the internet, if the wifi here is working." instructed Bob.

"Go." shooed Sheila, as she waved Bob off, before she headed toward the truck.

Bob returned in a few moments, and climbed back into the driver's seat. "What do you have?" he inquired.

"It's bad." frowned Sheila, as she folded up her laptop computer. "According to the radio, it's actually weird. There are reports of a hospital being overrun by people on some sort of drug-fueled insanity trip. And, they've left the hospital, and have wandered out on to the highway, where several of them have been hit."

"Ugh." griped Bob.

"But, here's the weird thing. Even though many of them have been badly mangled by the cars and trucks which have hit them, none of them have died. For that matter, they've continued their drug-fueled rampage, and have even attacked the ambulance crews attempting to help them. So, the cops have closed the road, until they can get the situation under control." explained Sheila.

Bob frowned. "Not good. Any estimate on when the road will be open again?"

Sheila shook her head, which caused her short, dark brown hair, unrestrained by a hair tie, to swirl around her head. "No, that's just it. They've lost contact with most of the officers out on the highway. Communications are all screwed up, and things are, apparently, out of control."

"I'm sure it'll make the front page of the newspaper tomorrow, but I don't intend to stay in this area that long." explained Bob, as he frowned again. After a quick look at the navigation display, he added, "Well, if the interstate is closed, we can try taking the back-roads."

"In this?" questioned Sheila. "I'm not sure we ought to take this beast down a little country road."

Bob shook his head, as he pointed to the satellite navigation screen, "No, I was intending to take secondary roads, but not the narrow country roads. See, if we take highway 23 north, until it intersects highway 48, we can take that to the west, and then take highway 27 south, which will get us around the blockage, and back on the interstate. It'll slow us down a bit, but it's better than sitting here on our hands."

Bob silently cursed. He had hoped that Sheila would sleep through the radio exchange. "Yeah, we'd better." he replied. "I've got an exit coming up in about three miles, and there's a truck-stop there. We can fuel up the beast, and find out what's going on."

Sheila giggled. "That suits me just fine. I'm beginning to feel the call of nature, and if I have to pee in a bottle one more time, I think I'll scream."

Bob sighed. While he certainly didn't want to waste the time stopping, he realized that it would be a good chance to refuel the truck, get some information on the nature of the highway closure, and to visit the restroom facilities himself. Truthfully, he was beginning to feel the call of nature, too, and he despised having to pee in a bottle almost as much as Sheila did, even though his anatomy made things a bit easier for him. "Yeah, I'll fuel up the beast, while you answer the call of nature, and then we can get some information about why the road is closed, as well as a grease burger or two." laughed Bob.

"Eww." grumbled Sheila. "I agree with everything, except the part about the grease burger. Maybe they'll have pizza or chicken?" she suggested.

"Hey, now, you know that truckers live on grease burgers." laughed Bob, as he spotted the exit approaching. He flicked on the turn signal, as he steered the truck onto the exit ramp, and then made the turn toward the truck-stop. "Doesn't look too busy. Maybe we won't be jammed up getting to the pumps?" he questioned.

"Yeah, looks pretty deserted." responded Sheila, as she climbed out of the sleeper section, and plopped down daintily into the passenger seat. "You'd think that if they had the interstate highway blocked that there'd be more trucks in here."

"I'm not sure I like this." stated Sheila, as she glanced around the lot of the truck-stop.

"Well, as long as we can get refueled, and get some information, it can't be too bad." replied Bob, as he steered the large blue truck, with it's silvery Aluminum box trailer into one of the pump lanes.

Bob nodded thoughtfully. "Yeah, I would have thought so. This place looks almost empty. That's weird. Most of the time, truck-stops are packed full of trucks for the night."

"I'm not sure I like this." stated Sheila, as she glanced around the lot of the truck-stop.

"Well, as long as we can get refueled, and get some information, it can't be too bad." replied Bob, as he steered the large blue truck, with it's silvery Aluminum box trailer into one of the pump lanes.

Bob set the brakes on the truck, as Sheila climbed out, and headed into the truck-stop. Normally, Bob would have accompanied her, just to ensure that no one tried to take advantage of a petite lady, although he pitied the fool who would try to cause trouble with Sheila. He knew that she could defend herself quite adequately. Still, he did have a touch of chivalry. But, he really did want to get the truck refueled, and resume his trip as quickly as possible.

Bob inserted his company credit card into the pump, and smiled as it registered it. He then pulled the large green nozzle from the pump and inserted it into the left-side fuel tank. He then walked around to the right side of the truck, and repeated the process. By fueling both sides at the same time, he could minimize the refueling time.

Bob shuttled back and forth between the left and right fuel tanks, just to make sure the pump would shut off automatically, and that he wouldn't spill a quantity of Diesel fuel on the ground, if the nozzle were to remain stuck in the open position. Finally, the left-size nozzle clicked off, and Bob hung it up on the pump, before replacing the cap to the fuel tank.

TRUCKING ZOMBIES

By Albert Moss

It was a dark and stormy night, with rain pounding against the windshield, as Bob steered the blue Kenworth semi-tractor down the desolate interstate highway. The lightning flashed in the distance, as distant rumbles of thunder made their way into the cab, while the big six-cylinder Cummins ISX 15-liter Diesel engine purred along. "Are you sure we shouldn't stop, at least until the storm subsides?" asked Sheila, his driving partner, from the comfort of the bunk in the sleeper portion of the cab.

"Nah. We've got to get this load delivered on time." replied Bob, as he shifted gears, as the semi-truck plowed through the water on it's way up the next hill.

"You just get some sleep. I've got another three hours of driving, before my time is up." continued Bob.

"Ok." sighed Sheila, as she laid back down on the lumpy bunk, and pulled a dirty blue blanket over her. "I just can't imagine what's so important about this load." she wondered rhetorically.

"Something about some kind of medical product." replied Bob halfheartedly. "And, you know how I feel about vaccines, especially after that nonsense about the last vaccine."

The truck bumped over a bridge, as Bob grumbled about the state of the highway, and how the promised infrastructure repairs never seemed to make the roads better. All they seemed to do was to cause construction zones, which backed up traffic. Bob yawned quietly, before he glanced down at the fuel gauges. The right side tank was empty, although the left side tank still had 25 gallons. Then, again, with the fuel economy the Kenworth W900L obtained, of 6.6 miles to the gallon, he realized that he was going to have to stop for fuel sooner, rather than later. Bob did a bit of quick mental arithmetic, and arrived at a range of about 150 miles before he was going to have to stop for fuel, which would take him about two hours, an hour short of his allowed driving time. Still, he realized that he didn't want to push on for too many miles, for fear of running out of fuel, since that would really screw up his schedule if that were to happen. And, he realized, the rain and wet roads may be cutting down on his projected fuel economy.

Bob glanced back over his shoulder at Sheila. The two had been driving together for several years. While there was nothing romantic between them, he often wished that there was. But, Sheila had made it clear that she had sworn off of men after her third divorce, and had no intention of becoming romantically involved with Bob, or any other man, ever again. Still, Bob recognized that Sheila was not only a competent driver, but also a very beautiful lady. Sadly, he shifted his eyes back on the road, as the highway markers sped past the window of the truck.

"Breaker 19" blared the CB radio in the cab of the truck. Bob quickly reached down, and dropped the volume level, so as to not wake Sheila, although he believed that she could sleep through anything. "Anyone out there on the super-slab got their ears on?" came the gravely voice over the radio.

Bob reached down and grabbed the microphone, and keyed the transmitter, as he replied, "Go ahead. You've got the Blue Dragon here."

"Blue Dragon, this is the Gray Goose. I'm up here at mile-marker 129, heading west, and we got us a problem. The smokies have the interstate closed. I've got flashing blue lights all over the place." came the voice over the radio.

Bob glanced out the window, and saw that he was passing mile-marker 105, which meant he had about 24 miles to go before he would encounter the highway closure.

A quick glance at the satellite navigation map showed that he had an exit coming up in three miles. While he didn't want to stop quite yet, he figured that it would be the prudent thing to do. That would allow him to refuel the truck, and to get some information on the highway closure. The last thing he desired was to come up on the blocked highway in a truck which was running low on Diesel fuel.

"You stopping?" came Sheila's voice from the sleeper portion of the cab.

EVENTS

Hang out with authors, grab some books, check out the process and meet other bibliophiles. Let's look at what we found.

May 2023

Gaithersburg Book Festival, May 20, 2023, Gaithersburg, MD.

June 2023

Book Lovers Con, June 1-4, 2023, Orlando, FL.

Readercon, July 13-16, 2023, Quincy, MA.

Nantucket Book Festival, June 15-18, 2023, Nantucket, MA.

Book Bonanza, June 23-24, 2023, Grapevine, TX

July 2023

Detroit Festival of Books, July 16, 2023, Detroit, MI.

Readercon, July 13-16, 2023, Quincy, MA.

August 2023

Mississippi Book Festival, August 19, 2023, Jackson, MS

Bouchercon World Mystery Convention, August 30-September 03, 2023, San Diego, CA

September 2023

Bumbershoot, September 1-3, 2023, Seattle, WA.

Carolina Mountains Literary Festival, September 7-9, 2023, Burnsville, NC

Printers Row Lit Fest 2023, September 9-10, 2023, Chicago, IL

Kansas Book Festival, September 16, 2023, Topeka, KS.

The Bookmarks 18th Annual Festival of Books & Authors, September 21 – 23, 2023, Winston-Salem, NC.

Washington Island Literary Festival, September 21-23, 2023, Washington Island, WI.

The South Dakota Festival of Books 2023, September 22-24, 2023, in Deadwood, SD.

Milford Readers and Writers Festival, September 22-24, 2023, Milford, PA.

The Brooklyn Book Festival, 25 September – 3 October 2023, Brooklyn, NY.

7. Do be clear on the things you liked or didn't like.

If you loved the book but didn't like the politics... This is not a reason to slam a book. Appreciate the writing talent and give props for that and note that it was a little too political for you. Politics in a book does not make for a one star review.

8. Don't leave false reviews.

We've seen reviews that had nothing to do with the book. The reviewer blatantly did not read the book. This leads us to the dreaded DNF review. "Book was so bad I couldn't eve finish it." Whammo, one star... But... how do you know? You didn't finish the book... It is best to just walk away and not leave one.

9. Do be honest in your review.

If the book was great but had a few grammatical issues, feel free to say so but it is not neccessary to sing to the rafters how good it was when it left you wanting in the end. Just reember to review honestly and try not to go overboard in either direction ont he minor issues and look to the overall book in your reive. What are the feels? Tell us that!

10. Don't leave a review for the sole purpose of torpedoing and author or book.

Finally, this is the worst of reviewers. Those who hop onto a book at the behest of someone or some perceived duty to another author. These reviews are just wrong and oh so very transparent. [can you hear the disdain in this?] This kind of sabotage is cruel at best. Authors spend sometimes years working to bring their story to life Leaving a one star review because of comma usage is... Well let's call it what it is. A low down attack on another person and should not ever and we mean EVER be done.

Unfortunately in the indie world this is becoming more and more an issue, the tearing down of one another is never beneficial.

Remember to always be kind and read on Friends!

2. Don't leave a spoiler in your review.

Even if you loved the book, if you drop a huge spoiler in your review, you could inadvertantly ruin the experience for another reader or worse yet, make it so that a reader wont buy because there was no reason to read.

3. Do mention the things you liked.

If you just loved the fact that the main character has some flaws but overcomes them in an epic way. Mention how relatable the character was. Because after all, don't we all have things to overcome in life? It's what makes life interesting.

4. Don't make your review biased or subjective.

We all have favorites, don't we? Favorite authors, favorite tropes, favorite genres. Sometimes this favoritism can lead to subjective opinions both good and bad that add no value to the review. When we do this we are inserting our own opinions as opposed to what the book really is which is the one thing we are complaining about in the book. Ironic huh?

5. Do offer how the book made you feel.

Were you affected by the story, did it leave you in tears or make you angry when the antagonist bested the hero. Were you emotionally drawn to the ally for the hero. Our favorite ally is Samwise Gamgee and the way he is faithful to the end to Frodo.

6. Don't level insults or abuse.

There may be times when books can be outrageous or different than you are used to, perhaps the language is harsh. The characters may not align with your beliefs or sensibilities. Writing an abusive review does not offer anything to the potential buyer. If you don't like a book you can say so without being rude, it will add credibility to your reviews.

READERS: DO YOU REVIEW?

TEN DOs & DON'Ts OF REVIEWING

If you're one of those readers who take the time to review books, you're a gem!

Authors love reviews and not only do they love to read them and get your feedback, but they help the algorhithms figure out who is enjoying what books.

But did you know there are some finer points to reviewing that authors would very much love for you to know.

Following are the Dos and Don'ts of Reviews that every author whishes all readers knew!

1. Do take a moment to leave that review.

No matter what, even if it is just a few words to say you liked it, go ahead and do the author a solid by dropping that review. Being an author is quite similar to operating a business. Just like any other business, reviews help in building integrity and credibility among the readers. It also attracts new readers, and positive reviews encourage them to buy your book.

The criers of the publishing world will tell us that the e-book and self-publishing is the harbinger that threatens the end the paper book. It is said that "within 25 years the digital revolution will bring about the end of paper books."(Morrison, 2013) Anguishing that e-books will put an end to writing as a profession. It is incredibly short sighted to think that moving into the digital age will equate to an end to books. An excellent example is, "Haven't future projections been wrong in the past? Didn't they say Penguin paperbacks would destroy the print industry in 1939? That the printing press would overthrow Catholicism after 1440? That home videos would destroy cinema?"(Morrison, 2013) As we move into a digital age we must compete with video games and Netflix, as writers we too must evolve. Many indie authors have cracked the USA Today's top 150, and many more make a decent living from their efforts. Admittedly though, it is those who possess a strong entrepreneurial spirit that can pursue such endeavors with the most success.

The world of words is fraught with examples of writers, excellent writers, which went largely undiscovered for lengthy periods because of the haphazard ways of the publishers. There is now a massive network of all forms of indie arts that all work together and have successfully challenged the status quo. The resources outlined, and others show a clear correlation between self-publishing and a change in the publishing world. Highlighting the ways authors can make this work for them is one way to outline the options. Showing the ways authors can benefit both monetarily and with intellectual content helps them make an informed decision. Finally, it becomes an option for the little-known author to expand their readership.

In conclusion, the argument that Indie authors are not real authors is based upon outdated resources and flawed information. In showcasing the differences between both, highlighting the pros and cons of each will provide the writer the relevant information to determine which route is the best choice for them. Authors who ignore self-publishing options suffer because, many who have blazed the trail have had enormous success. By seeking and contributing to the support of other indie authors, they cannot only benefit but contribute to this emerging digital era. There is a clear bias in the world of authors, a bias exhibited by sources such as the NY times best sellers list. The only way to change this is to become better writers and create works that, like Edgar Allan Poe, who had to self-publish his first works, can challenge the status quo.

Resources on the subject

http://angryeaglepublishing.com

https://www.forbes.com/sites/georgeanders/2014/07/...

https://www.theguardian.com/books/booksblog/2016/m...

http://www.selfpublishinghalloffame.com/

http://authorearnings.com/report/february-2017/

http://www.creativindie.com/how-much-does-book-edi...

http://www.indiebooksbeseen.com/#/

Works Cited

Donahue, Deirdre. "E-books Are Already Creating a Self-Publishing Revolution." E-books, edited by Debra A. Miller, Greenhaven Press, 2013. Current Controversies. Opposing Viewpoints in Context, Self-published Authors Find E-success," USA Today, 13 Dec. 2011.

Morrison, Ewan. "Digitizing Books Devalues the Work of Professional Writers." What Is the Impact of Digitizing Books?, edited by Louise I. Gerdes, Greenhaven Press, 2013. At Issue. Opposing Viewpoints in Context, Are Books Dead and Can Authors Survive?" Guardian, 22 Aug. 2011.

Options like editorial services and cover art are available from other indie artists and other non-traditional avenues. Companies like Quiet house editing can edit and format the book, for a fee of course. This fee can cut into the author's profit margin, as can fees for illustrators and cover art. The difference is that the author chooses who to have edit it and how much. Beta readers come from many places and some will read an author's book in exchange for a read of theirs. Organizations like Indie Books Be Seen and Association of Independent Publishing Professionals, assist indie authors with these services. These are new and emerging services and ones where groups are banding together. Self-publishing means that the author is paid upwards of seventy percent of the royalties on their works, (amazon, n.d.)

While the average royalty share for the author of a book traditionally published is a mere fifteen percent. This has been the traditional standard based on things like cover design, editors, typesetting and distribution when they were much more laborious. (Anders, 2014) The downfall being with self-published works is that now the author must secure these services. Some might say that self-published books have errors or are not as high of quality (and for some this is true), but lately with publishers using editing software, mistakes are not caught before publication from even the best publishing houses. Here we have a real example of ways the author can increase their earnings and see much more of their royalties.

A company has recently emerged, Angry Eagle Publishing Group. It is one that connects author/editors with others, matches producers with rights owners on audio books where there are options for exchange of services can be an option, as opposed to royalties being chipped away. In this model other authors also showcase their peers in social media and other advertising avenues, offering access to multiple avenues available to them. This highlights the point that they can not only influence but control the creative process, while still maintaining a sizeable amount of their royalties.

While Angry Eagle is still a traditional royalty paying publisher for some books, other options remain to best suit the needs of the author and the work. Under this new model they allow authors to choose their publishing options with varied options. Ranging in options offering prepaid packages, traditional royalties models, and ala carte services to fit the needs of each. Even now many traditionally published authors, for many reasons, find themselves seeking to go the self-published route and struggle for the rights to their own work and further show the reasons authors might choose this route.

Some great authors were turned down by publishers, and self-publishing is often a means to showcase otherwise overlooked authors and works. Some like Lord Byron, T.S. Eliot, Zane Grey, Ernest Hemingway, Edgar Allen Poe, and even Mark Twain were turned down by traditional publishing. While most of these well-known authors are now published traditionally, at some point they too were self-published. One such author Michael Prescott, after being turned down by 25 publishing companies decided to self-publish his thriller Riptide. He now finds himself among one of the fifteen self-published authors who cracked the top 150 on USA TODAY's Best-Selling Books list in 2011. (Donahue, 2013) The point of which is that "Today, authors such as Prescott can bypass traditional publishers. They can digitally format their own manuscript, set a price and sell it to readers through a variety of online retailers and devices."(Donahue, 2013) By highlighting the ways other writers, who have blazed the indie trail, have overcome the obstacles, we can now benefit from their efforts. The misconceptions surrounding the publishing industry are arguably many. The goal is to sort out these and argue in favor of the self-published author and provide facts that show how the indie world has progressed.

The Indie Author
Much Ado About Self-Publishing

Writing in the indie world is an uphill climb. Many excellent writers, glorious storytellers with magical mysteries flowing onto pages, are never seen. Manuscripts being sent for review with high hopes. The only response received… rejection after rejection. Dashing hopes, and sometimes silencing dreams for good, these struggles plague many authors.

by DJ Cooper

There is quite an argument surrounding those who choose the indie route, claims that they are not real writers or vanity published. The argument goes further to contend that writing is not a real career, except in the rarest of cases. Writing in all forms and more specifically the novelist can indeed, not only a career but a rich and fulfilling one. Self-published is not vanity publishing, on the contrary, it is full of possibly the hardest working authors out there. In vanity publishing you pay someone to publish and distribute your works but an indie must wear many hats. From writer to editor, cover designer to publicist; the indie does it all.

Overcoming the stigma of the indie author, and with it offering a view into the real world of the indie artist offers the best way to persuade authors to trust in themselves and not give up. Writers are the hardest ones to persuade on this topic. They have very definite ideas about what an au-thor is, it has been one of the largest misconceptions in the realm of the author, and for some, it seems set in stone. Some say there is a difference between an author and writer. Using the logic that states, a person is a writer until a publisher accepts their work, then and only then can they call themselves an author.

Authors should not discount self-publishing; in it the author retains control of the work and the financial gains, it is a means to showcase otherwise overlooked writers and their works. Often, publishers retain larger parts of the money for not only their profit, but to cover expenses of professionals used in the final publication of the book. Authors struggle to make a profit on their arduous work, averaging only about fifteen percent royalties. Yet, even with professional editors, publishing companies can still have published books with major errors. The resources available to writers that have been traditionally provided by the publisher are not as limited as publishers would like them to believe.

With amazing stories they tell the tale of the end. Find within the pages ideas on how to use preps, ways people improvise, and what one might face in a grid down or end of the world scenario while you enjoy a good read.

Join in the antics

HEAD OVER TO THE FACEBOOK GROUP TODAY!

- *BIRTHDAY FUN*
- *GIVEAWAYS*
- *BOOKS*
- *AUTHORS*
- *FUNNY CHATS*
- *VIDEOS*
- *DISCUSSIONS*

Come on in and sit a while, the authors came to chat all things zombie

APOCALYPSE ANYONE?

Have you joined our apocalyptic reader group? Interact with authors, find books, discuss the end of the world and preparedness.

https://www.facebook.com/groups/writtenapocalypse

MEET THE AUTHORS OF THE APOCLYPSE

- DJ COOPER
- JENN AMATO
- STEVE HEUZINVELD
- CASSADIE ROSE
- AJ NEWMAN
- JEFF MOTES
- SM LITTLE
- DEREK SHUPERT
- MILLIE COPPER
- DA CAREY
- BARBARA GILBERT
- ROB VANDERSYS
- RAY WENCK

We want to highlight the mastermind behind this event!
STEVE HEUZINKVELD

When the country descends into chaos, how far will you go to survive?

No news. No emergency services. And the governor just fled the state.

When Riley Armstrong's father comes home early wearing his police uniform, she knows something is wrong.

Only a handful of people are aware of an asteroid that is threatening to turn the West Coast into a crater, but it's only a matter of time before everybody else finds out.

Her grandmother's farm is fifteen hundred miles away from the impact zone. But with anarchy spilling into the streets, and lunatics at every turn, will they even survive the perilous interstate journey to get there?

Officer Keith Bowman, a hard-headed brute serving a suspension, runs point for his partner through the city. But when what's left of his broken family falls apart, and it's everybody for themselves, is anyone worth saving?

Facing moral dilemmas and unique challenges on every leg of the journey, Riley and her family are forced to do whatever it takes to survive.

The first book in The Fall series - Plunge into an apocalyptic thriller with everyday characters thrust into an explosive high-octane action adventure.

https://www.amazon.com/dp/B0BQZ6CK58

$11.99 Paperback
$3.99 Kindle

WORDPEDDLER MAGAZINE

THE CONTENDERS

Voting begins in the apocalypse group September 2023

Steve Heuzinkveld - Survivors of The Fall
https://www.amazon.com/dp/B0BQZ6CK58

Peter Wood - The Steading
https://www.amazon.com/dp/B0B3532KLT

Jenn Amato - The Group: Jana
https://www.amazon.com/dp/B0B9ZF5QBC

Terry Grimwood - Deadside Revolution
https://www.amazon.com/dp/B01LZG3HJI

Cassadie Rose - Expiration Date
https://www.amazon.com/dp/B08DK4J3W6

Charles Banning - The Dead of Night Chronicles
https://www.amazon.com/dp/B0BRJST7LC

S. M. Little - Slow Collapse: Beginnings
https://www.amazon.com/dp/B0BYW-51W8Y

Cal Brett - Worse Than Dead
https://www.amazon.com/dp/B08MV8H5N5

Boyd Craven III - Blackout: Still Surviving
https://www.amazon.com/dp/B079R2C6B3

EE Isherwood - Neighborhood Watch: After the EMP
https://www.amazon.com/dp/B09BG4VPXH

Don A. Carey - Goose Truman: The Horsemen
https://www.amazon.com/dp/B093TRG7YB

Tara Ellis - Point Of Extinction
https://www.amazon.com/dp/B08SBVTFFN

Austin Chambers - Venom Spear: Blades of Grass
https://www.amazon.com/dp/B09N3BYCBG

Chuck Rogers - Bastard of the Apocalypse
https://www.amazon.com/dp/B07VMVM-

DJ Cooper Endure the Chaos https://www.amazon.com/dp/B09Q3KZR3P

Damien Lee The Virus https://www.amazon.com/dp/B08ZG7MHTY

Millie Copper Caldwell's Homestead: Havoc in Wyoming https://www.amazon.com/dp/B07YN78JWZ

John O'Brien A New World: Chaos https://www.amazon.com/dp/B004W0CL2Y

Robyn VanDerSys Black Hills Fall https://www.amazon.com/dp/B09TS1DNDN

David Kazzie The Immune https://www.amazon.com/dp/B07RVDCNL4

Derek Shupert Survive the Fall https://www.amazon.com/dp/B08B5538FN

Scott M Baker Nurse Alissa VS The Zombies https://www.amazon.com/dp/B087PY5NBJ

Kyla Stone Edge of Collapse https://www.amazon.com/dp/B07Y3XS2KY

Kate Morris The McClane Apocalypse https://www.amazon.com/dp/B00JM-1GY0S

AJ Newman Old Man's War https://www.amazon.com/dp/B09L79F3DY

Jacqueline Druga My Dead World https://www.amazon.com/dp/B06ZZS6K2T

Ray Wenck Random Survival: The Road https://www.amazon.com/dp/B07KY4JS-DG

David Saylor As The Light Dies https://www.amazon.com/dp/B0BQX1DN1H

Jeff Motes Once Upon An Apocalypse https://www.amazon.com/dp/B01N1RKPP3

Lindsey Pogue The Darkest Winter https://www.amazon.com/dp/B07Q1WZJ57

APOCALYPTIC BATTLE ROYALE

- DJ Cooper - Endure the
- Damien Lee - The
- Millie Copper - Caldwell's Homestead: Havoc in Wyo
- John O'Brien - A New World:
- Robyn VanDerSys - Black Hill
- David Kazzie - The Im
- Derek Shupert - Survive th
- Scott M Baker - Nurse Alissa VS The Zon
- Kyla Stone - Edge of Col
- Kate Morris - The McClane Apoca
- AJ Newman - Old Man'
- Jacqueline Druga - My Dead V
- Ray Wenck - Random Survival: The
- David Saylor - As The Light
- Jeff Motes - Once Upon An Apoca
- Lindsey Pogue - The Darkest W

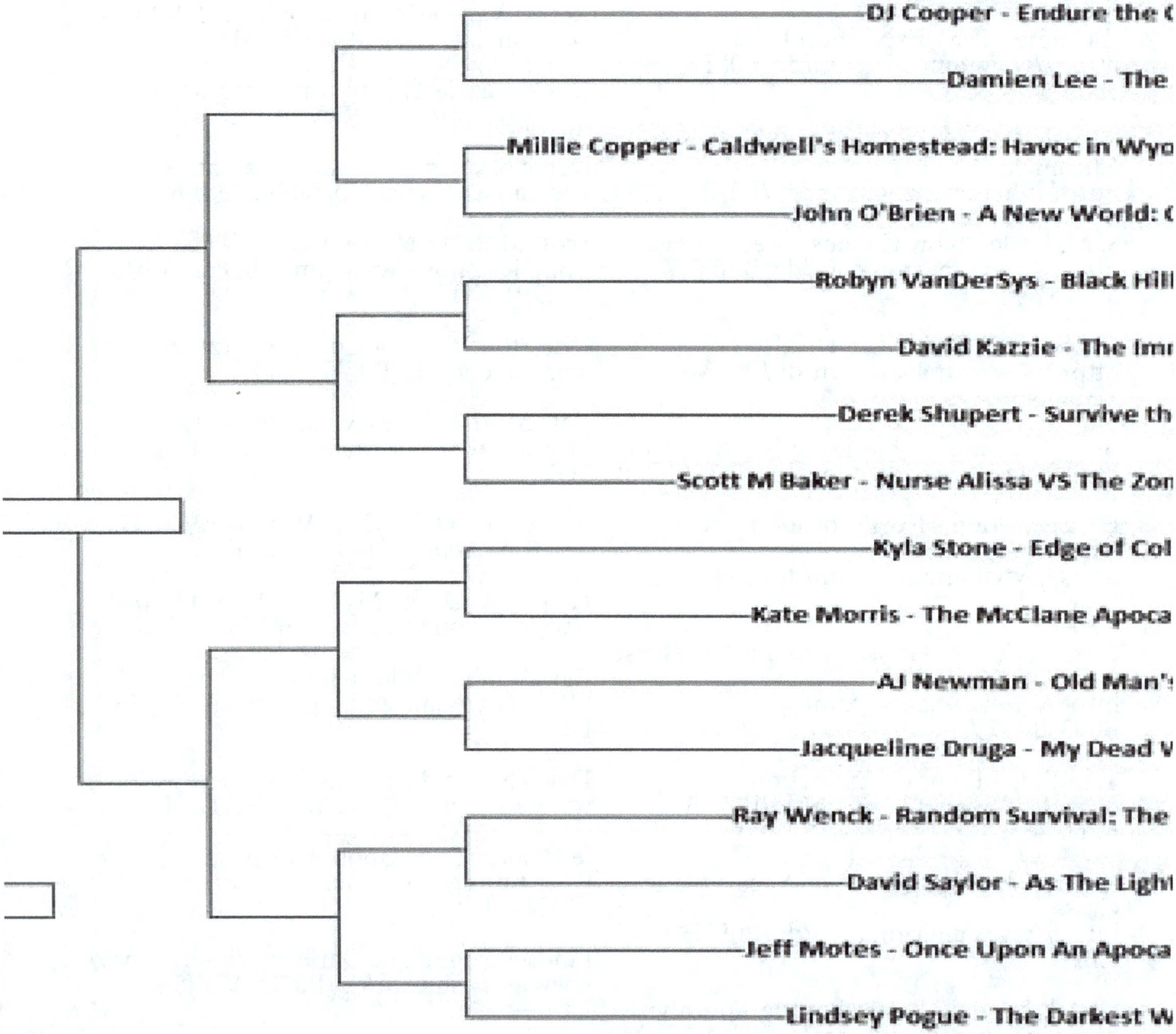

WA
WRITTEN
OCALYPSE

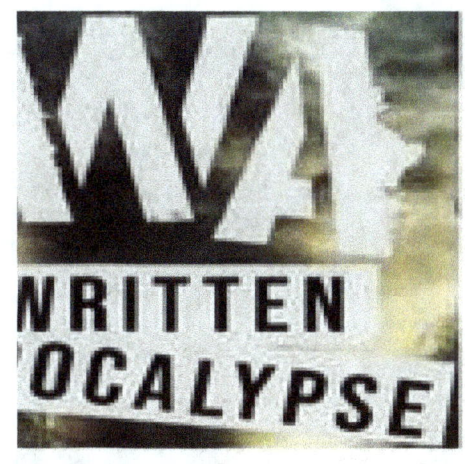

POST-APO BOOK BATT

euzinkveld - Survivors of The Fall
'ood - The Steading
nato - The Group: Jana
rimwood - Deadside Revolution
e Rose - Expiration Date
Banning - The Dead of Night Chronicles
tle - Slow Collapse: Beginnings
t - Worse Than Dead
aven III - Blackout: Still Surviving
wood - Neighborhood Watch: After the EMP
Carey - Goose Truman: The Horsemen
s - Point Of Extinction
Chambers - Venom Spear: Blades of Grass
ogers - Bastard of the Apocalypse
Gilbert - Future Apocalypse
ser - When The Dead Rise: The Outbreak

Winner

THE GROUP
A POST-APOCALYPTIC ZOMBIE ADVENTURE

BOOK 2 NOW AVAILABLE FOR PREORDER
HTTPS://AMZN.TO/3UZZ5RV

Find Her Books

No one is ready for this!!!

Jana expected a new life when she left the UK for the big city life of Toledo, Ohio. What she didn't expect... was to find herself stuck in the Midwest, newly sober, and fighting zombies.

ISBN: 979-8986923147
$11.99 Paperback
$3.99 Ebook
amazon.com/dp/B0B9ZF5QBC

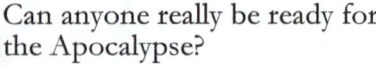

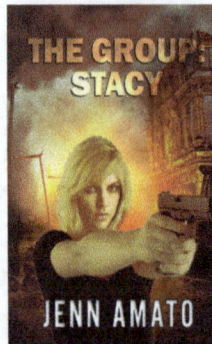

Can anyone really be ready for the Apocalypse?

The second book in The Group Series Stacy Is the person most likely to live as she helps this rag-tag group of misfits as they struggle to survive amidst zombies and humans that have no good intentions.
FOR RELEASE MAY 30,2023

$3.99 Ebook (preorder)
amazon.com/dp/B0B9ZF5QBC

Follow Jenn

Jennamatoauthor.net

Amazon
amazon.com/stores/Jenn-Amato/author/B0BBPTS6VN

Facebook @jennamatoauthor

Instagram @jenn_amato_author

WP: Do you have other things moving forwad that you are planning?

JA: After the third book, I have one more book to write, *The Group: Jason*. I will then challenge myself to write a sci-fi novel. I'm not sure if it will be a series. I have thought about crossing genres and broadening my horizons but that remains to be seen.

We've also discovered that this series of books will be the jump off point for a Fan Fiction world of books where other authors will be contributing stories that will tie into the world of *The Group*. Jenn was excited that Angry Eagle Publishing approached her with the concept and looks forward to working with other authors on their stories as well

learn more about *The Group World* and others through Angry Eagle on their website.

AngryEaglePublishing.com

Her latest book is on preorder for a May 30, 2023 release date.

A few facts about Jenn readers might like to know.

1. I own 2 small businesses, work a job, write, and help my friend with her small business.

2. I have 3 german shepherds that I treat like my children.

3. I have 3 grown human children and I am a grandmother of a 2-year-old who calls me "Nonna" which is Italian for grandma.

4. By the time this prints I will be married to a man I met in jail. Slow down, we both were Correction Officers and have been together for 8 years. My author last name is not my married last name.

5. I am spiritual and am into stones, crystals, herbal medicine, and astrology, and my business is based on herbal medicine for which I have gotten certificates to practice.

6. I can't spell.

7. If I had the money, I would be a prepper with a bunch of land and a bunker underground.

8. I LOVE CANDY!

9. I am an ordained minister.

10. I have such a filthy mouth, Orbit gum cant clean it up.

JENN AMATO

AUTHOR OF THE GROUP

On becoming an author.

Our featured Author spotlight is with Jann Amato who is the author of *The Group Series* of books. The WordPeddler asked her about becoming a first time author and about her life and writing.

WP: Tell us about why you wanted to become an author.

JA: I wanted to be an author since I was 14 years old. I started out reading Dean Koontz and have been hooked on horror since then. I read through most of his books that summer. My love of reading started even younger when I first started reading books like The Babysitter's Club. Writing didn't really become a reality until I met Jack Childress and started hosting podcasts with him. I was "nudged" by Jeff Thomson, Jack Childress, Richard R Rose, Angel Ramon, and James Dean to begin writing a book that turned into a series. I then solicited DJ Cooper, owner of Angry Eagle Publishing, to publish my book. Being published was one of my goals in life and on my 45th birthday, I was able to check that off my "to-do" list.

WP: Tell us about how you write.

JA: When I write my stories, I let them tell themselves. I write what plays out in my head and sometimes, I can't write fast enough as it plays out. My characters come to life and with my first series, the characters are based on real-life people.

WP: With post-apocalyptic stories the question everyone really wants an answer to is what does your browser history look like?

JA: [Laughing] My browser history looks a lot like a med student researching a paper on deadly viruses. In my book, I have managed to mix two nasty viruses that are out there and rare. I'm sure the farther I go in my writing career I will end up on a couple of watch lists.

WP: We all seem to have this issue at times with writing our books. As writers and most especially indie writers the other things seem to have a huge pull on our time. What things do you struggle with in writing your books?

JA: The biggest issue I have with writing at the moment is time. I just can't seem to find enough time right now to write as much as I want to. I also find that if I am tired, my creativity is stifled. It's hard at times to make writing a priority when I have so many things demanding my time.

WP: Tell us what you are working on right now.

JA: I am currently in the process of writing my third book, *The Group: Aaron*. This one is a bit different from the first two because they were based on real people. Aaron is not based on any people I know and is entirely made up. I did this to challenge myself and see how creative I could get.

'There, I think that should do it.'

'What now?'

'Now we wait, those other readouts will indicate whether any of this worked.'

'And if it doesn't.'

'I'm not factoring an alternative to success' Ben replied bluntly, 'Not after all we've been through.

The atmospheric nitrogen levels were rising close to their 78% along with 22% oxygen and trace amounts of CO2. The exterior temperature was rising but just slightly whilst readouts for the earth rotation rate were right on track.

Just then one of the monitors flicked to a relay feed of the President stood in the situations room surrounded by the secretary of defence and several CIA officials. Their skin was still spotted with the bark-like substance but it was slowly falling away.

'Who am I speaking to?' the President asked.

'Ben Walters sir.'

'Ah, and how old are you son?'

'I guess I'm around 23 now maybe more, I lost count after 'flare day' sir.

'Yes, yes I quite understand. I want you to know son you've done a great thing here today. You've reversed a global catastrophe and ensured the well-being of all mankind. Who is that young lady by your side son?'

'It's Kaylee sir, she's helped me throughout.'

Kaylee forced a smile though it was disingenuous at best.

'Son I think you can agree that playing digital gods has taught us a very valuable lesson.'

Ben nodded solemnly.

'That our next orbital reconfiguration program should be headed by you son, a true coding genius. Think of it son, this planet no longer orbiting the sun but joining the moons of Saturn, just think of the possibilities...

'The End ...

Ken Robinson began writing when he was 12 years old and has never looked back. He graduated from the University of Portsmouth with a degree in English and Creative writing and continued his writing education with evening classes at his local college. Proceeding that he wrote all things from short stories to novels to a few screenplays but found his passion in the novel/novella field particularly in the genres of horror and fantasy with the subjects mainly continues writing to this day chasing that elusive traditional publishers mantle so he can move one step closer to making this not just a passion but his full time career.

A book that refused to give an inch and took miles of my thought process. Although it is fiction much of it ran parallel to biblical occurances that only an open mind will appreciate in the fierce and horrifying chain of events leading to the war against the Great Dragon. Mythology, Atheism and Christianity all intersect for a very involved read. - Amazon Reviewer

FIND KEN ON AMAZON
HTTPS://AMZN.TO/45F7ONB

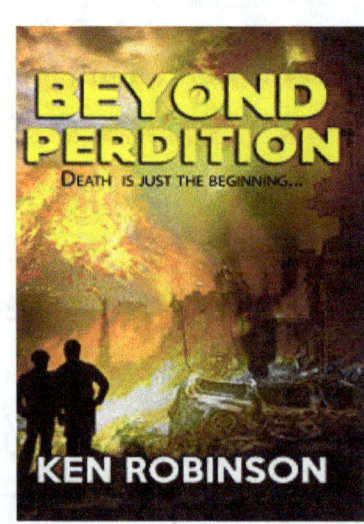

Kaylee wiped her eyes 'I want this damn thing to be over, I want to see my mum again and everything to be back to how it was before.

Ben led the way out of the room, his bladed weapon still unsheathed his other hand gripping Kaylee's. If the core server unit entrance would be anywhere it would be somewhere that the President had access to, he was after all the most powerful person on the planet especially since presiding over America basically made one a top ranking leader in the new world order according to the long established governmental hierarchy.

History classes, at least those Ben had attended had explained much of how a singular global government was still run by the leading economic (as well as host of other factors) countries on the planet. He never knew this information would ever come into use until now as he finally stood in the oval office holding Kaylee's trembling palm in one hand the fate of the world in the other.

14

'I don't know what we're looking for.' Kaylee said pulling her hand away and surveying the ornately decorated interior.

'I think it will be as simple as a basement door.' As Ben explained this he stepped carefully on the carpeted floors feeling and listening for any differences that might give away a concealed hatch. He was quickly losing hope when Kaylee trod in an area that squeaked.

Using the bladed weapon which had proven more than useful at this point, Ben sliced into the carpet, the blue material coming away to reveal exactly what he had hoped for. A concealed entranceway leading straight down.

They wasted no time as they both entered the newly availed opening and found themselves descending a gradually sloping tunnel. Ice cube tray lighting ran the length of the slanting ceiling whilst a network of intricately connected piping, dials and valve wheels occupied the walls left and right.

'You okay?' Ben asked as they were nearly an hour into their descent.

Kaylee shrugged, 'It doesn't matter if I'm okay or not, let's just do this.'

A second hour elapsed and gradually the tunnels were getting hotter despite several large air con units occupying space between the arterial piping.

'We must be nearing the core. Ive seen plenty of labelled pictures of the server farms and hive monitors so I'm hoping I'll be able to find what I'm looking for quick.'

Kaylee didn't reply, her head a million miles from this overheated subterranean tunnel system.

The server room was much larger than Ben had imagined from the images he'd often poured over. It was unreal to be stood here when it felt like only yesterday he was analysing low res digital images of this place. The noise was deafening like a perpetual thunder or a never ending earthquake. Between the technological obelisks were the consortium of monitors. A veritable display of universal codes moving like neurons inside a giant brain.

Ben ran to the nearest screen and tried explaining what he was seeing over the deafening din. 'It's all here, orbital trajectories, atmospheric composition regulators, tidal cycle manipulation codes.'

But can you fix this?' Kaylee shouted.

Ben typed into one of the many lines of keyboards below the monitors. As he did so he mumbled to himself, something he had often done when back home writing codes.

'It's one of the original coding languages that superseded binary. The planets polarity is expressed in conventional longitudinal and latitudinal coordinates. Spatial mathematics should make it possible to switch back the polarities thus righting the axial positioning of the planet. When these things are off kilter, the train comes off the track, reset to how they were and I can re-establish the original orbit. We're be exactly where we need to be in relation to the sun.'

Kaylee watched distractedly as all around them the servers and the generators buzzed and hummed like angry hornets.

'It may take a little time to notice a difference. The earth is one big mass and turning it in any direction is like turning an aircraft carrier round in the ocean, it's done gradually and carefully.

'That would only result in being chased by ten or more armed guards unless you're suggesting...' Ben stopped himself as he clocked the sincerity in Fowler's face.

'One of us is going to have to be the distraction and I am fully aware what that means.'

'You can't they'll shoot you on the spot. We know that no survivor groups since 'flare day' have ever trusted outsiders, they wont think twice before killing you.''But it will give you and Ben time to get in unseen. This is bigger than us it always has been. Sure I want to find my brother, I want to see him well again but in order for him to even get well, for your mum ben, and yours Kaylee, I need to do this. Think of it as my calling.' There were tears in his eyes even though he was making the effort to smile 'Anyway try living life as half a tree, hard wood syndrome hey Kaylee?'

'Don't do this Fowler, we'll work out another way. Give it a little time, Ben's smart, smarter than both of us, he'll figure it out.'

Ben surveyed the grounds. Although it looked as if the guards all followed a rigidly set routes they had all areas covered, there was no getting through.

As if he could read Ben's dismay, Fowler shot from their crouched positions and ran head on towards the patrolling guards.

Kaylee went to follow but Ben pulled her back harshly, his voice now slightly above a whisper. 'If you reveal yourself now then this would have been for nothing.' As he spoke there was the sound of rapid gunfire and screams cut short.

Ben was forced to hold Kaylee's wrist tightly and pull her towards the perimeter fencing. The guards had descended upon the perceived intruder and as hoped had not noticed them breaching the outer defences and heading towards the rear of the building.

Kaylee's cloying sobs were much louder now the gunfire had ceased. She was shaking so badly she could barely stand. 'He didn't have to do that, he didn't have to do that,' She sobbed, 'Why the hell didn't you think of another way? There had to be another way, there had to be.'

Ben picked at the lock with the tip of his bladed weapon and to his utter surprise managed to unlock one of the doors. Dragging Kaylee inside he closed it firmly.

'There may be more guards inside, you need to stay quiet.'

She removed her NBC suit helmet and revealed that same tangled, unkempt hair Ben had seen on 'Flare day' but unlike the cold and resilient look she had had back then, her cheeks were shiny with tears and her lips quivered as if they being cruelly manipulated by an outside force.

'I'm sorry Kaylee, I really am, he was good guy.

'He was more than that' she cried, he was my...' her voice was again lost to uncontrollable sobs.

13

They did not move for quite sometime. Ben tried his best to console her but his own guilt at not coming up with an alternative plan of action made it hard to formulate the words. Fowler had been with them from the beginning and though he didn't possess the psychic kinship, he was part of their family after the event.

' Let's finish this for him' Ben said eventually.

Kaylee looked as if she were going to argue but as she managed to steady her breathing she said in a hoarse voice 'Sometimes we would go out scavenging together and he would tell me about what he and his brother would get up to. They were proper pranksters but they were good people. Nothing that's happened so far should have happened to them, not if there still is a God here, the way Fowler thought there was.'

'He was a deep thinker at times,' Ben agreed, 'Sometimes he'd surprise me with profound thoughts seemingly out of nowhere. I've been a practical thinker you see. I've never really be able to think in the abstract. But I know from the many nights we've had in the shelter, Fowler was primed to do something great, and I believe this was that thing, let's finish it for him.'

11

Kaylee had argued that if God still existed then he would have intervened whilst Fowler in one of his rare moments of intellectual debate claimed that God was letting everyone see the consequences of their actions, that this was some kind of karmic justice for playing at being something we had no right to be. When Ben was involved in the conversation the next morning he decided to reserve judgement in favour of a peaceful day. He knew the road would be long and that though they were still relatively early into their journey they were already becoming sick with the dehydrated rations and the tasteless water.

As they re-entered the built up areas more of the 'rooted' showed themselves between the detritus of fallen high-rises. 'Help us children, help us.'

It was hard to ignore their pleads for help but necessary if they were to continue their mission successfully. They covered around twenty miles a day, resting for six hours a night and hitting the road again in the early morning hours. It was cooler in the morning and less likely they were going to meet any more kids. It seemed for the most part, the children of other areas all held that same infantile fear of the dark, something they just never grew out of. Ben admittedly still found it very unsettling but whenever he was worried he would clasp the hilt of his bladed weapon ready to draw it out at a moment's notice.

The days were uneventful, until the green rain reappeared and sent the party running for cover. It pelted it down hitting the stone eaves above them and eroding the concrete below. They reluctantly huddled together in narrow doorway of what may have been a high-rise. They could not enter inside as the structure was roofless, the only protection coming from the stone protrusion at its entranceway.

Ben watched as the green droplets cascaded down and burned through the bonnets of the cars and buses and formed fizzing pools on the road.

'Screw this' Kaylee exclaimed, 'We could be stuck here forever, might as well be one of those tree things, it's not like we can move.'

Ben bit his tongue, he wasn't about to indulge her complaints, not today.

Fortunately the downpour lasted only eight hours which compared to the deluge back at the shelter was short-lived. The damaged wrought however left them speechless. Had they been caught in it, even for a few seconds, their NBC suits would have been as useful as silk leotards. Even when they stepped out they had to tiptoe between pooled areas where the rain had yet to corrode straight through the tarmac.

It was a relief when after a further two days of about 45 miles covered the group saw signs reading 'Washington DC ten miles'.

The niggling doubt was usurped by the absolute need for this to be right. If they could locate the Whitehouse, find the entrance to the core server units and hack into its central processor with new instructions to reset the polarity of the planet then the orbit and everything adverse that came from altering it would be fixed. It sounded too good to be true, but Ben would be damned if he weren't going to at least test this theory, it wasn't like anything could get any worse.

12

The Whitehouse was still standing. They couldn't believe it. Even the heavily manicured front lawn continued to look immaculate. But if Ben and company had thought that they were just going to waltz straight in they were sadly mistaken. Though all CIA and other secret service operatives had long been turned into the 'rooted' a number of child soldiers had taken up the mantle of guarding the last bastion.

Ben counted at least ten each holding M-16 rifles and patrolling the front and side entrances.

'There's no way we're getting through there' Kaylee whispered. 'And I don't fancy our chances negotiating with them.'

'We won't need to,' Fowler suddenly said, 'We draw them out, simple distraction.'

'   Look' Ben said pointing at an old parish, its lead roof still intact. Outside, stood as still as the gravestones in the cemetery were a number of 'rooted' they looked as if they had been quite a bit older when flare day had happened. Their postures were bent forward, their limbs gangly and now they had the same curvature as a series of miniature weeping willows bent over the banks of a river.

'It's horrible' Ben remarked. 'Probably just came out of church and bang, that happened.'
'We all suffered' Kaylee interjected, 'I still maintain it's harder for those who weren't infected, we have to find ways to survive in a world that quite frankly isn't survivable any more. They at least don't need to eat or...'

'How can you say that? Ben erupted, surprising even himself. 'I would never envy their situation and nor should you. Damn it how can you be so cold? It doesn't make sense.'

'She's not being cold,' Fowler interjected, 'She's hurting, we all are, we're going through the five stages of grief even though our loved ones aren't actually dead.'
Ben smiled despite himself 'Well Fowler that has to be the most profound thing I've heard you ever say. I didn't think you had it in you.'
Fowler shrugged, Kaylee marched ahead not wanting any part of this emotional nonsense.

They had reached the coast by nightfall and figured they would have to redirect their travels in land if they were to reach their destination. They travelled the first half of the night with the group arguing the validity of Bens calculations, bearing in mind his map reading sofrware was proving less than accurate. Ben made a few rebuttals but decided he was going to leave out the findings on the tablet, at least for now. Even he had to admit that the niggling doubts were growing larger. Was this a futile mission or could something really be done about all of this?

10

Ben's mums face seemed to fold in on itself as the white light hit it. Ben ran through the living room and out of the hallway, stopping only when a girl ran passed, her hair scruffy and tangled. He followed calling after her until they reached the outside and were simultaneously blinded by the glaring light. When their vision returned they could make out the full scale of the carnage. Most of the surrounding buildings had toppled to the ground, thick dust clouds spiralling out of the rubble. The usual bleeping car horns had ceased with all the vehicles' occupants frozen in poses of fear and confusion.

'Where now?' Ben asked

'It's not like I have this figured out. You probably know this city better than me anyway, my mum only moved with me last year to get away from my dad.'
Ben looked across the street trying to figure out where they would go, how they would get there and what they would do once they did. It was a chaotic train of thought that was interrupted by a loud wailing.

'It's coming from that car' Kaylee said pointing to one of the smoking vehicles on the furtherest lane. Ben instinctively ran over. There were two people seated in the front. One had been transformed completely and was merely folded forward onto the dashboard like a crash dummy. The second however was very much alive but something stood out. His arms were covered with the same bark like growths...

It was quite a relief to Ben not to be woken up for the remainder of that night. Fowler and Kaylee had stayed up arguing on the existence of God and where all this fit into the biblical accounts of the universe. Both Fowler and Kaylee had only been given sparse accounts from the texts during history lessons in school. It was common knowledge that all bibles were burnt in 2538 AD during a triple sixer revolution and the forming of a one world government. Historians had maintained that the tech age followed this with humans taking things into their own hands.

8

When Ben awoke it was to Fowler staring down at him.

'Mate you're quite the snorer, it's your time to take the watch, I wanna get some kip.'

Ben looked up at the ominous moon whose curdled light was spilling over the natural pathway weaving between the cornfields and farmland. From this point he could make out the faint silhouettes of silos slanted over deserted barns and old cottages.

He sat down by the small fire Fowler had managed to create and powered on the tablet. He had managed to find some old cell batteries in the shelter to prolong its lifespan. The owner had left some encrypted word documents but it was so basic to decipher that Ben was reading the first page within twenty minutes. It was a survivor account, another child's rendition of events.

'Ever since the light flash the headaches have got worse. mum and dad have both turned, I'm not sure what to do. Before dad turned he was working on code. It made no sense at the time but he was dead proud of it. He sent portions of it to me as a way of explaining what he was working on but I'm no programmer. In leman terms he was writing orbital code, something about changing the trajectory of the earth he said it was all connected to some core server but like I said it means nothing to me. I'm relaying this in case I meet someone who can make sense of it all. I don't want to forget anything he said to me. I don't know if its connected to anything that's happened but it doesn't take a genius to figure out that altering a planet's orbit is probably not a great idea....'

The entry stopped before several paragraphs of coding language filled the page. It was in the same language as Ben had seen on the core service hive monitor but this time it was instructional. It was a means by which the poles, north and south were being reconfigured to turn the axis of earth in an alternate direction. The processing power involved was immense but judging by the events of 'Flare day', maybe this had all been a success (if success was the right word).

Kaylee came over to sit by the fire. 'Go on get some more rest' she said, 'Sun up in three hours.' Somehow though she was telling him what to do which was not out of the ordinary her tone was calm almost comforting.

9

The wind had picked up the next day blowing dirt from the road into the air in thick clouds. Kaylee admitted several hours in that she had only once ventured further than the farmlands and so couldn't recall what they were going to encounter next. Fowler was on edge as his rough skin had been irritating him and although not subject to 'psychic flashes' he was convinced someone was following them.

Towards evening with the group walking the entirety of the day, the ground sloped down into what appeared to be a village. Detached houses lining cobbled streets and an ominous quietude pervading the place.

'Damn this is surreal, its like we're in England or something' Fowler remarked, 'Where the hell are we?' he looked at Kaylee when he asked this.

'Beats me but let's keep our guard, where's there's houses, there are most likely people looting said houses.'

Ben's Geiger counter beeped loudly. 'I think we're entering a pocket of high radiation, make sure you rely solely on your respirators here.'

The cobbled streets and flagstoned side-walks were particularly wide, made more noticeable by the sheer lifelessness of the place. It was like it had been frozen in time but not this time. There were no technological trappings, no street side servers no phone charging points or transport repair bays. It was almost medieval when compared to the scientifically advanced cities.

'It's fine' Ben said, staring at a row of the 'rooted' poking out of the rubble like paralysed spirits. There's farmland beyond the city, less people in rural areas and less…' he pointed towards the stone obstructions.

By the time they had reached the outskirts of the city, the natural day and night cycle free of artificial programming had turned the sky into a navy blue and dispersed the clouds to reveal an enormous moon shining down like a Cyclops's eye.

Up ahead, there's a crew of them lying in wait, they haven't seen us yet, at least I don't think.'

Then lets take another route.' Fowler said pointing down an alley containing the burned out remains of numerous restaurant wheelie bins. They they ran through into another district where raised office blocks formed a sequence of brick obstacles and blockades.

What do you see? He asked as he saw her wincing with the pain of the telepathic revelation.

"Up ahead, there's a crew of them lying in wait, they haven't seen us yet, at least I don't think.'

'Then lets take another route.' Fowler said pointing down an alley containing the burned out remains of numerous restaurant wheelie bins. They they ran through into another district where raised office blocks formed a sequence of brick obstacles and blockades.

'Great' Kaylee remarked 'Just what we need.

'It's fine' Ben said, staring at a row of the 'rooted' poking out of the rubble like paralysed spirits.

'There's farmland beyond the city, less people in rural areas and less…' he pointed towards the stone obstructions.

By the time they had reached the outskirts of the city, the natural day and night cycle free of artificial programming had turned the sky into a navy blue and dispersed the clouds to reveal an enormous moon shining down like a Cyclops's eye.

7

Ben was exhausted when they reached the outskirts of the city. They agreed to rest by a copse of actual trees devoid of faces and screams of anguish and settled for the night taking turns to look out.

The garishly bright white light issued through the window of the shaking apartment block and struck ben's mother's face with such ferocity the light seemed to disperse over her features and burn into her skin. A moment later only her eyes could move as her skin became like petrified wood covered in nodules and ridges of hard bark.

Ben ran for help, diving through the living room and out the door into the hall way. The building continued to shake, ceiling bulbs crashing to the floor in glass confetti. A girl ran out into the hall as well. She couldn't have been more that 16, her hair unkempt as if someone had rubbed a balloon on her scalp. She had a large diamond earring which stood out in stark relief from her sooty face. As sped passed Ben, he noticed she was wearing a t-shirt with a horrifically maimed raggedy Ann doll skewered on a pike.

'Hey wait up' ben cried, 'Where you going? What's happening?'

'Darned if know. I'm getting the hell out of ere though.' she began descending a stairwell taking two steps at a time.

'Did you see the light?' Ben called after her

'Couldn't bloody miss it, thing turned my mum into…

Ben wanted to reply but his voice was lodged in his throat and he was finding it hard to keep up with her.

When he could at last speak he said 'Are you sure it's even safe outside? I mean maybe we should wait here, wait for help.'

'You do you' she replied curtly 'but I ain't sticking around. Whatever that was could get us next.'

'What's your name? Ben asked between rapid inhalations.

'Does it matter?'

'Well I'm following ya so it might come in handy.'

'Fine, it's Kaylee.'

5

'Don't you get it guys? This explains everything.'

Kaylee and Fowler appeared bemused bordering on uninterested.

'So what if it does?' Kaylee asked 'Not like we can do anything about it now.'

Fowler seemed to agree with her sentiment as he scratched at his hardened skin. 'Just accept what is done, it's easier that way.'

'But don't you see, the problem has been isolated, that means the next stage is a solution.'

Noticing that he still had the floor Ben continued 'If I can find the core server unit and rewrite the orbital codes I could steer the planet away from the sun, it would alter the strange weather, it could even…'

'What?' Fowler asked suddenly sounding interested.

'It could reverse what's happened to our loved ones, in the right conditions it might reverse the inflictions and bring them back.'

Even Kaylee couldn't ignore this startlingly revelation. If Ben was right then perhaps her own mother and Fowler's brother, not to mention countless others could be returned to the world of the living. 'Flare day' had been thought of as the apocalypse, as the end but perhaps it didn't have to be, perhaps there was an epilogue to all of this.

Fowler filled up a gas can with treated, deionised water whilst Kaylee stitched any loose seams in the NBC suits. They wasted no time in rationing the MRE supplies for a long journey, dividing the ration packs into their heavily modified satchels. Ben headed outside and spoke with his mum, this time confidently assuring he had the answer.

Respirators and masks packed, Geiger counters reconfigured and strapped to their hips alongside an assortment of med kits, bladed weapons and trekking systems in case they got separated, and they were ready to set off.

Even while they were speaking Ben had explained his theories on the position of the core server unit. It would be in a centralised location with an entrance obviously accessible on the surface so it would not be at sea and by his calculations it would be located in what used to be geographically known as the United States of America, Washington to be precise, right where the Whitehouse used to stand.

6

Ben's mum looked as if she were going to tear up at the news that this could all be reversed. Her eyes leaked a fluid, not clear but red and viscous, trailing down her oaken front onto the irradiated earth below. Even Kaylee usually against anything which made her think of the event was in high spirits. They knew they at least had a week's window before another deluge of the green rain and judging by the other charts they were not going to encounter any sun flashes which occurred when the remnants of programmed cloud cover dispersed in areas where the ozone layering was also depleted. Kaylee knew the area at least for the initial leg of their journey whilst digital maps that Ben had programmed to update in real time would show some kind of lay of the land even if it were mere rudimentary topographical data.

The air was cold the morning they left. The group, all helmeted at this point, communicated through a radio system using the call signs where possible. The hardened soil under foot crunched as they collectively passed the sporadic copses of 'rooted' and headed to where the city had once stood. It was an awe inspiring sight even on the hundredth time. Subsumed masonry littered the eviscerated tarmac. Downed phone lines crossed streets strewn with vehicular carnage. The cars were all stripped anatomical, engine blocks stolen, petrol siphoned, and wheels long gone. Other children had been here. Their survival instincts leading them to loot and pillage, to raid and ransack. Smashed store fronts with dismantled awnings margined the business districts whilst pubs and clubs had been left in smouldering mounds of rubble.

Kaylee stopped. She clutched her forehead, Ben knew exactly what this meant.

'Great' Kaylee remarked 'Just what we need.

Ben shrugged, 'Wasn't here when I woke up.'

'Great you tried him on the comms, the stupid plonker's probably still looking for his big brother. Wouldn't be surprised if he's a puddle of skin on the floor by now.'

'That's not funny' Ben moved across into the small comms room which separated the sleeping quarters from the rec room. A long panel of controls fronted a bank of monitors. Weather readings, radiation readouts, and a reconfigured sonar device designed to detect movement in the global forest all surrounded the comms unit. Ben picked up the mouth piece 'Delta one four this is eagle six eight do you copy over?' A carbonated crackle followed, 'Delta one four this is Eagle six eight do you copy over?' Kaylee had joined Ben's side, her eyes moving across the readouts.

'This is Delta one four receiving over.'

'Where the hell are you Fowler?'

Ben shot Kaylee a glare, 'Don't use real names over the radio, what if the other groups are listening?'

Kaylee rolled her eyes, 'Whatever man, just triangularize his location or whatever you do cos it's unlikely he's gonna know exactly where he is, whole forest looks the same.'

'I've just crossed the tech glade over.'

'Roger that, over and out. There you go' Ben said 'twenty minutes and he'll be back. I knew you missed him.'

'Shut your mouth' Kaylee said punching Ben in the arm hard, 'That will be the face next time.'

4

Fowler returned with several pelts and a small rectangular device. Discarding the pelts at Kaylee's feet just to annoy her, Fowler passed Ben the device. 'Found it in the tech field, thought you might be able to make sense of it.'
Ben still couldn't help but stare at Fowler's arms. He had been seventeen on 'Flare day' with just three months to his eighteenth. As a result the infliction had hardened some of his skin, turning him into a kind of half tree, half man hybrid, a phenomenon Kaylee had jokingly called stiff wood syndrome.

'It's a tablet,' Ben said, 'Very similar to the one I used to use before...' he stared pensively at the control panel. 'It was in the tech glade you say?'

'Yeah under all the other mounds of junk, actually found it under a catchers' mitt of all things.'

'It still has some residual power, yeah, I might be able to do something with this, thanks.'

'Nerd' Kaylee said.

Many hours later as the wind howled outside the bunker carrying the chorus of voices from the 'rooted' into the night air Ben set about retrieving the contents of the tablet. It was redundant binary mainly but some JPEGS of the core server were among the picture files. That was when Ben noticed something he had never seen before. A static data stream on of the core server hive monitors. To anyone else it would mean nothing but as Ben used a substitution code and recalled one of the many now redundant universal programming languages he could make out a message that horrified him to the core. horrified him to the core.

It was not in fact a list of instructions, often the case as long infected programmers left operating notes to assist in the continuation of Earth's primary functions but a note, a singular journal entry which read thus:

This is it, there's no going back now. In trying to save the human race we have doomed mankind. The orbital reconfiguration programming is sending us too close to the sun. the consequences will be dire. This is the end, farewell.'

The note abruptly ended and was followed by small embedded codes for stratospheric protection but nothing Ben hadn't seen before.

2

Ben woke with a start. It was the same recurring nightmare, the same memory of 'flare day' which haunted all who had lived to witness it. He could hear a loud dripping and looked up to see that the green rain had finally corroded a hole in the metallic panelling comprising the shelter's roof. 'Damn it' Kaylee would be out on a supply run and Fowler, well Fowler was of little use in this situation. He'd have to do a quick fix. Weld secondary panels to the compromised sections and check that none of the generators had been affected. It would be catastrophic if they couldn't power the air purification units or the water filtration systems not to mention it would affect the recalibration of the Geiger counters that were so heavily relied on with the unpredictable atmospheric radioactivity.

Any fatigue had lifted the moment Ben had mentally compiled the list of things to action. The rain was definitely heavier now and debatably more acidic. It seemed to hiss as it hit the shelter floor and continued through the very crust of the earth. It would of course be worse for those who were outside. Kaylee would have found shelter but there was no such protection for the 'rooted'. Ben ran across to one of the quadruplicated window panes and stared out at the forested stretch before him. It would be easy to mistake the numerous spindly boughs and gnarled limbs as nothing but ruined forestry but each narrow trunk rooted permanently to the ground was once a living, breathing person. And the one closest to the shelter's entrance was none other than his mother moved and planted here at her own request.

The solar flare had been fast and purposeful. It had turned all whose aged skin was too old, too compromised to resist the sun's burning attack that fateful day into things resembling burned husks or as they were later termed the 'rooted' due to the hard bark-like appearance of their flesh and inert quality of their limbs. Only those under the age of 18 had survived, but not unscathed. Ben still suffered periodic migraines and something Kaylee had once described as 'psychic flashes' where, for the briefest of instances, she and many of the other surviving children could communicate to each other through the forest of the 'rooted'.

'Flare day' had been almost ten years ago. There were few buildings left standing, and most of the solar radiated land had been turned into a bleak vista peopled by those that made up a giant global forest. Parents, older siblings, uncles, aunties, grandads and grandmas all rooted to the ground in postures reminiscent of their final moments. What was maybe worse was that they could all still talk and constantly bemoaned their situation, urging those who had survived to find a cure and end their suffering.

Though their faces had aged and creased, many beyond recognition, the skin of those who had escaped that fate did not seem to change. They did not grow older and so they became colloquially known as 'Children of the end.'

3

'That bloody rain nearly got me,' Kaylee cursed as she stripped out of her makeshift NBC suit and entered the small jury-rigged decontamination unit which fronted the shelter. 'Why didn't you radio me? Give me a heads up. It's not like you couldn't have predicted this.'

'I was sleeping sorry.' Ben jumped down off the ledge soldering iron in hand 'At least the shelter should last a bit longer. Meteorological readings say there shouldn't be another green rain incident for a week or so.'

'Well whatever. Not like your computer readouts did me much good this time anyway. I got some more MRE packs from the military base, won't taste great but I fancy that over any animal contaminated by the rain. Where's Fowler?'

DIGITAL GODS

By Ken Robinson

Ben scrolled his finger across the tablet. It was an ancient device, didn't even use TPST chips (telepathic software tech) but since the last power outage it was the only remote digital unit he could access. The digital diagrams were not immediately obvious in their low res pixilated form but he knew well enough what he was seeing. The angular features of the crowded server farm, the many archaically powered auxiliary generators still running on petrol, an expensive, unreliable fuel source at best. The hive like formation of monitors outputting code in reams of nonsensical data. Or at least nonsensical to those 'unenlightened'.

Ben saw the streaming numerals as more than a random consortium of digits but as instructions. Instructions that controlled all other server units on the planet. As he had often tried to explain to his 'unenlightened' parents the 'core server', named for its position in the Earth was essentially in control of all factors pertaining to the continuation of human existence. Its inventors had termed it the 'Human Preservation Program' or HPP. It was a series of code written to circumvent the laws of the universe and override the governing algorithms birthed at the genesis of the cosmos. It would, in theory, manipulate or perpetuate ideal weather conditions to ensure sustainable agriculture. It was set to alter the tidal effects of the moons gravitational pull to better control oceanic activity. It was even meant to reconfigure Earth's orbit around the sun to reverse the costly effects of global warming.

It had achieved most of this and its semi-open-ended server networks had meant that Ben was able to contribute his own code in the race to improve on nature's grand design. Of course now with his own computers down the coding had ceased and the program to divert rain clouds would have to be put on hold. Still, there was something soothing about looking at the technological marvel that was the 'core server' base, the hub of existence, the brain of the universe.

'You in bed yet?' Came an angry voice from behind the bedroom door. ' I don't want you being cranky tomorrow cos you didn't sleep.'

' I'm in bed,' Ben lied, powering off the tablet and staring at the multiple high-rises populating the metropolitan skyline. The twilight sky functioning under the 'diurnal cycle code' was painting the heavens mauve. He couldn't sleep now, not with the power down, not when his mind was racing with unwritten, unpublished, uncredited code.

Suddenly the room shook. The tablet fell from his hands as several loose computer components joined it on the already cluttered floor. Mum burst in, her complexion as white as the light that now appeared beaming through the window. Ben watched on in horror as the woman who seconds earlier had moved with the speed and agility of a startled rabbit was stood statuesque, her frozen pose accentuating a final scream of agony. Her skin especially along her arms and hands was no longer white but the brown and scabrous texture of bark leaving her to rigidly resemble the leafless limbs of a long dead tree.

We'll leave the door open for you! Just remember to respect the rules and be kind.

SOCIAL GROUPS

No matter which genre you love there is a group that will offer fun interaction with authors and other readers

Who doesn't love hanging out chatting books with other fans and the authors themselves. Find some of your favorites right in our own network of groups and start socializing and finding new reads. Search for them on Facebook and join today!

Just the books!

Post-Apocalyptic & Prepper Reads

Scifi, Fantasy, and Horror Book Club

Fan Groups — Genre

WrittenApocalypse — Apocalypse

WrittenUndead — Zombie Fiction

Asylum of Fear — Horror Fiction

Spicy Books — Romance/Erotica

Fantastic Magical Worlds — Fantasy Fiction

Dystopian World — Dystopian

Written Sci-fi — Science Fiction

The Ops Centre — Spy Thriller

More coming soon...

For the Authors

Authors of the Apocalypse

WOW- Writers on Writing

Dauntless Cover Design

WORDPEDDLER MAGAZINE
What's inside

- 6 Find the Groups
- 24 Post-apocalyptic Battle Royale
- 28 Meet the Apocalypse Group
- 30 The Indie Author
- 33 Do you Review?
- 37 Book Events
- 50 New in Books
- 52 Meet the Zombie Group
- 55 Apocalypse Acronyms in books
- 56 ETOW Recipes
- 58 Book Listings
- 70 Apocalypse Wordsearch
- 92 Editor's Picks top Apocalypse books

The Editor's Desk

Our anthologies and other projects that sought to bring words to the readers are such amazing ways to showcase the new writer that we wanted to bring you more. Not just a book of stories but highlights from your favorite authors, new releases, sales, contests and so much more.

Writers of short works seem to get the short end of the stick sometimes, so we wanted to not only bring you the goodies in this space but the amazing talents shown in the blink of a few pages, along with poetry, and whatever else tickled our writing fancy.

The challenge of creating an entire tale in a set amount of words [often not many at all] is daunting. Describing the place, the people, the issues and struggles and folding it all in at the end for a perfect closure to a tale is no easy task and should not be taken lightly.

Welcome to the WordPeddler, the Peddler of words and stories.

Remember to share your favorites with others and review.

Independent authors must wear many hats and you, the reader, can help.

See you in the pages!

DJ Cooper

Featuring

08
Digital Gods
A Short Story
by Ken Robinson

38
Trucking Zombies
A Short Story
by Albert Moss

72
One Second Advantage
A Short Story
by N.A. Broadley

81
Writer's Corner
Psychology of Character
by Jeff Thomson

84
You're Never Too Old
A Short Story
by Christi Reed

20

WordPeddler Author Spotlight
Interview with

JENN AMATO

On The Cover

08 Digital Gods
20 Author Interview- Jenn Amato
38 Trucking Zombies
50 Pre-order Releases
58 2023 New Releases
72 One Second Advantage
92 Top Apocalyptic Books - Editor's Picks

Copyright: 2023 Angry Eagle Publishing, LLC , North Walpole, NH. This publication may not be reproduced, either in whole or part, in any form without written permission from the publisher.

Printed in the USA

WordPeddler Magazine is a registered trademark of Angry Eagle Publishing, LLC

WordPeddler's Society

Mission Statement – The WordPeddler's Society is a literary foundation who's goal is first and foremost to strive to help readers find books they love.

WordPeddler's Society is a free service that helps millions of readers discover books they'll enjoy while providing publishers and authors with a way to drive sales and find new fans.

To support the professional development of independent authors by offering opportunities to collaborate and share one another's books, create a community of our peers, and offer help in the form of charitable options to get authors going.

Our goal is to build an organization with a focus on bringing stories to readers through community.

Consider following on social media and joining our website https://wordpeddlersociety.com

DJ Cooper

Editor

WORDPEDDLER

May/June 2023

AUTHOR INTERVIEW

Jenn Amato

Author of *The Group* series of books talks about becoming a first time author.

SHORT STORIES

Digital Gods
by Ken Robinson

Trucking Zombies
by Albert Moss

One Second Advantage
by N.A. Broadley

TOP APOCALYPTIC BOOKS

Editor's picks for books that started it all for us in the apocalypse genre.

PRE-ORDER

May/June coming releases

2023 NEW RELEASES

New in books
Apocalyptic books released in 2023

READER MAGAZINE

APOCALYPSE
EDITION

HOW TO SURVIVE THE ZOMBIE APOCALYPSE

wordpeddlersociety.com